HIDDEN NATURE

UNCOVERING THE UK's WILDLIFE

Dedicated to my wonderful father.
May your cheeky grin, green fingers and love for all
creatures - great and small - live on in the pages of
this book.
(I like to think you would have dozed off
in your armchair with it, too.)

HIDDEN NATURE

UNCOVERING THE UK's WILDLIFE

ISLA HODGSON

WHITE OWL

AN IMPRINT OF PEN & SWORD BOOKS LTD.
YORKSHIRE · PHILADELPHIA

First published in Great Britain in 2018 by
PEN & SWORD WHITE OWL
An imprint of Pen & Sword Books Limited
47 Church Street
Barnsley
South Yorkshire
S70 2AS

ISBN 9781526708922

Printed and bound by Replika Press Pvt. Ltd

Design by Paul Wilkinson

Pen & Sword Books Limited incorporates the imprints of Atlas,
Archaeology, Aviation, Discovery, Family History, Fiction, History, Maritime, Military, Military
Classics, Politics, Select, Transport, True Crime, Air World, Frontline Publishing, Leo Cooper,
Remember When, Seaforth Publishing,
The Praetorian Press, Wharncliffe Local History, Wharncliffe Transport,
Wharncliffe True Crime and White Owl.

For a complete list of Pen & Sword titles please contact
PEN & SWORD BOOKS LIMITED
47 Church Street, Barnsley, South Yorkshire, S70 2AS, United Kingdom
E-mail: enquiries@pen-and-sword.co.uk
Website: www.pen-and-sword.co.uk

Or
PEN AND SWORD BOOKS
1950 Lawrence Rd, Havertown, PA 19083, USA
E-mail: Uspen-and-sword@casematepublishers.com
Website: www.penandswordbooks.com

Contents

Foreword..6

1: COASTS...9
    The seal of approval (Seals)...12
    The Isle of Canna (Seabirds)..21
    The Big Friendly Giants (whales and dolphins)..................27
    A Duel on the Dunes (dune systems and sparrowhawks).....36

2. FRESHWATER...53
    The Montrose Basin (estuarine wildlife).........................56
    The Otter Family..65
    Swallows and Martins...73
    Wetland: A Refuge in the City..80
    Dragons Great and Small (ospreys and insects)...............87

3. THE LAND LOVERS: INLAND HABITATS.........................99
    Glenmuick (red deer)..101
    The Ghost of the Moors (hen harriers and moorland wildlife).....112
    A Species in the Red (red squirrels)..............................128
    Things That Go Bump In the Night (bats and owls)...........137

4. URBAN SPACES...149
    City Slickers (foxes)..151
    The Graveyard That Is Still Very Much Alive...................161
    Gardens Part 1: Feathered Lessons (garden birds)...........167
    Gardens Part 2: Marvellous Minibeasts (garden insects).....179
    Encouraging Wildlife To Your Garden............................189

A Final Word...191
Thank You..192

Foreword

For a book about wildlife, this one had a pretty unusual beginning. It all began with a taxi driver.

Throughout my zoological career, whenever people learnt what I had studied at University, most of their default responses were always the same: 'So ... you want to work in a zoo, then?' Perhaps it was the misleading word 'zoo' in the title, or maybe I just look the type. But if I had a penny for every time that my job prospects as a zoology graduate were confined to the limits of an animal's cage, I'd be a very rich zookeeper indeed. It was this exact conversation – this time in a taxi that was shuttling me to Newcastle central station for the beginning of another university term in Scotland – that started the idea for this book.

My taxi driver was an incredibly nice man, albeit a little ecologically misinformed. He was very concerned about my future. If, he asked, I was not going to work in a zoo, what on earth could I do with my degree? I ventured my ambition to become a conservationist. Eyes narrowed, he processed this information, before announcing that I would have to emigrate because – as he informed me, with the utmost certainty – there was "no wildlife in Britain". Horrified by this declaration, I spent the rest of our journey trying to convince him otherwise. But he had grown up in India, where the 'wildlife' were large, poisonous, brightly coloured, and in possession of sharp teeth and claws. For him, the word held entirely different connotations.

I pondered this as I stepped out of the taxi and onto my train. Rattling up the scenic east coast I thought back to conversations I'd had, with close friends and new acquaintances alike, about wildlife and conservation. Everyone gets excited about the big, enigmatic mega-fauna of our planet; outraged by the relentless poaching of elephants in Africa, or saddened by the victimised polar bears of the Arctic. People love to witness the fearsome prowess of a tiger stalking the jungle, or become enraptured by the charm of an orangutan in the rainforests of Borneo. All this excitement and interest is, of course, fantastic; these species are critically endangered, and need our help and support. But here in Britain, we are sometimes guilty of forgetting about the wildlife closer to home. Often, we don't really know or understand much about it at all, or even know just how much we have. It's easy to see how. The majority of our native species tend to be shy and elusive, relatively small, and well hidden. A rhino stomping around your garden is slightly difficult to ignore, but British nature has a much quieter approach.

Spotting some wildlife in the UK (as I will probably say a million times, consider this a pre-warning) is a true labour of love; requiring patience, dedication, and a healthy dose of luck. There are a few of us weirdos who will hang about in hides for hours on end staring at a patch of reeds or bog, just for that one sighting. But it can be hugely rewarding. And it doesn't even have to be that hard! We have a plethora of beautiful, enthralling animals right on our doorstep. A whole other world to explore. There are territorial stand-offs taking place on your bird table to rival those of the African Serengeti, and courtship displays so detailed and elaborate they put birds of paradise to shame (well, almost). Our hedgerows and meadows are our very own rainforests, our coastlines a treasure trove of natural wonders. We have fierce predators that stalk the skies, one of the biggest fish in the world patrols our seas, heart-wrenchingly cute critters scamper about the undergrowth of our forests and our gardens are filled with insects of every size, shape and colour. Underneath an upturned stone, nestled in the banks of a river, high in the rafters of your attic or hidden in the depths of a tree trunk ... wildlife is everywhere in Britain, if you just know where to look.

And that was the purpose of this book. Sitting on that train watching the coastline flit past my rain-streaked window, I decided to embark on a little mission: to write about our under-appreciated wildlife, in the hope that I could enthuse others to get passionate about it, too. I wanted to show that our flora and fauna can be just as exciting, just as dramatic ... and you don't need a degree or anorak to find it. I may have a PhD in 'conservation science' but when it comes to spotting wildlife I am still very much an amateur. Many of my encounters occur almost by accident, and I learn new things about the natural world every single day. There's also a sense of childlike curiosity to it, that thirst for adventure. To poke your nose into every nook and cranny, to see everything with wonder and excitement, to revel in being outdoors and not stuck behind a laptop screen. What you hold in your hand is a collection of stories, detailing my encounters with wildlife (intentional or otherwise) – the adventures of a conservationist who never grew up.

The book is split into four sections that cover what constitute, in my opinion, our main habitat types: coasts; freshwater; inland areas (forests, grasslands, mountains); and urban spaces. Within these four sections are chapters about the wildlife I've been lucky enough to come across there, and at the end of every chapter I've included a wee section that details how you might find those species or habitats, too; the best places across the country to catch a sighting; where applicable how to encourage these animals to your local patch; and – perhaps most importantly – how we can help them. This last point was the real drive behind writing this book. Many of our native species are declining at an alarming rate, suffering due to climate change, habitat loss, urban development and the intensification of agriculture ... amongst a multitude of other things. And, even worse, many are disappearing relatively unnoticed. I quickly came to realise that conservation only works if other people understand and love nature, too. In such a dangerous time for the natural world – when it is threatened from pretty much all sides – we all have a responsibility to protect it. In a way, we all need to become conservationists – whether you're a zoologist, a farmer, a builder, a student, a journalist ... or just someone with a little bit of time on their hands.

But how can we know what to save, if we don't know what we stand to lose?...

So here it is, my guide to re-discovering Britain's hidden wildlife. I hope you enjoy reading it as much as I enjoyed the adventures I took to write it, and that it inspires you to step outside the door and seek out just what the natural world has to offer.

Hackley Bay beach, Aberdeenshire. The beach is backed by dunes and sheltered by cliffs. The area is also known as Sands of Forvie.

COASTS

Being a small island in a very big world can have its benefits, one of which being we are never more than a few hours' drive from the nearest coastline. They may be close to freezing for much of the year, plagued by gale-force winds and flocks of hungry-eyed gulls that will steal your sausage roll before you've even had chance to look at it, but they also boast some of our most charismatic wildlife. You can almost guarantee a sighting of some kind of beastie on a wander down to the beach – whether it be a seabird, mysterious shell-dweller or a wee hint of something larger lurking beneath the waves.

If you are brave enough to endure them, our coastlines can offer some of the most breath-taking views; ruggedly beautiful landscapes carved out of the headland by saltwater, undulating sand-dunes that stretch on for miles. Such landscapes can be havens for wildlife. Geographical marvels such as stacks and arches – crafted by the sea through erosion – can be home to some of the largest colonies of seabirds in Europe. Occupying almost every ledge, stuffed into every nook and cranny or divebombing into the crashing surf below, they will announce themselves in a great cacophony of noise. Inter-tidal rock pools are treasure troves of rubbery beadlet anemones wafting their burgundy tentacles, and nippy little hermit crabs. Estuaries – where the mouth of a river meets the sea – often prove to be some of the most biodiverse areas in the British Isles, supporting not only larger birds and mammals but also vast quantities of tiny invertebrates that are vitally important to the health of the whole ecosystem. And, of course, there is an entire mind-boggling world beneath those waves, of which we can only catch a glimpse. The beauty of it is that there is so much about this world that we still

don't fully understand. On a planet where we can find the answer to most things at the simple click of a mouse, there is something about the unknown that is pretty special.

The North Sea – in particular the north-east coastline – has featured heavily in my life. Living in a seaside town on the outskirts of Newcastle, I grew up a true water baby swimming in the steely grey waters, exploring rock pools, surfing ... I spent my childhood and teenage years wind-swept and tasting salt water. Later I moved to Aberdeen for University where the Scottish coast was a mere ten-minute walk and discovered scuba diving, becoming addicted to the secret world beneath the surface, and when life became stressful the beach was always my escape. As a result, I have had some of my favourite wildlife encounters by the sea – whether that be beside, on top of, or under it.

Our coastlines provide ample opportunity for wildlife spotting; accessible, a rich variety of habitats and variable conditions. There is a great deal to see, most of the time without needing to look too closely – as I hope this chapter shows. Just make sure to pack your thermals...

Grey seal.

The seal of approval: the Ythan estuary

Seals have played a significant part of my zoological career. I spent a very enjoyable stint as a 'marine zoologist' for an aquarium that overlooked the mouth of the Tyne, which involved caring for four fully grown grey seals as well as rescuing any injured adults and pups that washed up on the beach below. Seals were also the focus of my dissertation, and for one happy summer in fourth year I sat on a beach, observing the behaviour of the enormous colony that inhabit a place called the Ythan estuary about thirty minutes' drive north of Aberdeen. Perhaps it has something to do with my attachment to dogs – to whom seals are so undeniably similar in character – but I formed an instant fondness for the soulful eyes, rolls of blubber and happy-go-lucky nature of these creatures.

Seals are a familiar feature of our coastlines and can be found in great numbers, lolling about on beaches and exposed sand bars at low tide, sunning themselves (well, on the odd occasion the sun is out) or interacting with one another in throaty, guttural voices. There are two species native to the UK; grey and harbour. Grey seals are generally larger in size, with sloping, roman noses and v-shaped nostrils, giving them a regal, disdainful air. They are certainly the more numerous and bolder of the two, forming huge colonies on small rocky islands just offshore or popping up in shipping ports, snorting loudly and waiting expectantly to be fed. In contrast, harbour seals (or 'common' seals, as they are also known) are more shy, exist in smaller colonies, and tend to be slender with a lighter colouring. They have the classic – or as some might say 'cuter' – Labrador face; large, baleful eyes and a short, whiskered snout, and seeing one lounging about on a rock can melt even the steeliest of hearts.

The Ythan estuary is the ideal place to study seals in the wild. Part of Forvie sands local nature reserve, it is home to one of the biggest populations of seals in the British Isles – although accurate counts are difficult to come by, the last estimate exceeded a thousand. And they're not hard to find. Rounding a corner through the sand dunes, a wall of mottled grey greets you accompanied by a symphony of grunts, groans and howls – you could almost be forgiven for thinking a drunken football crowd is awaiting you instead. Where the river Ythan opens out into the sea, hundreds and hundreds of individuals are hauled out on the sandbank, all jostling for space ... it's quite something. And for every seal on land, there are another ten in the water. At first, spotting them is a little like a game of 'Where's Wally',

The enormous seal colony at the Ythan mouth.

The wide expanse of Forvie sands with the nature reserve behind.

as their colouring is perfectly blended to the steely grey waters. But once you spot one, suddenly lots of little dome-shaped heads become apparent, eyeing you with a calm indifference. When you first encounter this vast, sprawling mass of pinniped bulk, your brain almost can't compute it.

Forvie sands is one of the few places you can get so close to such an extensive colony of seals, which makes it the prime location to observe their behaviour. They're so perfectly placed; on the sandbank of the nature reserve where humans are forbidden from treading, they remain undisturbed, separated by fast-moving body of water. But you can see them clearly from the adjacent bank, which kindly has tall sand dunes for an even better view. Stand for long enough at the water's edge, and the seals' natural curiosity will get the better of them – they'll come as close as three feet to snatch a good look at you. So once you get over the assault on the senses that is a thousand-strong colony of mammals, you can begin to appreciate their lovable personalities.

Seals are certainly fans of the slower pace of life. Most frequently found relaxing on the beach, like portly sunbathers, they don't do

things particularly enthusiastically. Their most energetic behaviour is to stretch laboriously, bending their back so that head and flipper meet at the top. Apart from this, they will lounge and laze to their hearts content, surveying the world around them with a glazed expression or lying with their eyes shut. Seals are very meditative to watch, and often remind me of a big group of blissed out bums at college, lazing about in their dorm room quite happy just doing nothing. My two course mates and I would sit in our little pop-up tent with binoculars eagerly fixed on the colony, and whole hours would pass by without anything really happening, to the point where it began to get a little frustrating. Most of the time, they either rested or drifted in the water with the current. Even scanning – in which individuals look around intently, searching for predators – was decidedly lazy in its execution, with he or she blinking slowly in one direction, and then the other, before settling back down into staring at nothing.

You may wonder what on earth I'm moaning about. Surely it must be quite a nice existence, chilling out on a beach whilst studying an animal that doesn't do anything hugely complicated? If you are

wondering this, you've clearly never visited a beach in Scotland. Most days we were battered by the wind and lashed by the rain, and sat frozen and miserable willing the seals to do anything interesting, just to make our numb fingers and wind-burnt faces worth it. The ordeal was made slightly worse by the fact that our meagre budget had only stretched to a two-man tent, and as a result we had to take it in turns to enjoy its warmth. The unfortunate soul sat outside had to make do with a waterproof 'dress' we'd fashioned out of a bin-bag, as if we didn't look weird enough lurking in a tent on a busy beach, with binoculars. So, on the occasion a seal actually moved with purpose, it was a very exciting event. Sometimes one or two would make the cumbersome journey across land, hobbling across to a new spot and providing some well needed comedic value to our day. Seals are not blessed in the walking department and so must shift about awkwardly on their stomachs, almost 'hopping' about on their bellies not entirely unlike deflated space hoppers. Even more exciting would be when such ungainly pursuits involved one male picking a fight with another. Bulls can be enormous – weighing up to 250kg – and therefore fights can be impressive. Roaring and grunting at each other, two males would roll about the shallows, reaching back to snap at their competitor; bashing their heads and flippers together as they locked in battle. However, these fights were brief and often ended as quickly as they had begun. The lesser male would give in, yawn, and return to the beach for a well-deserved nap.

Perhaps the most exciting event of all – the gold dust of seal behaviour, if you will (please forgive us, zoologists are exhilarated by the weirdest things) – was a 'flushing out' response. Forvie sands is an incredibly important area for seabirds, and the main side of the reserve is closed off to the public for the breeding season. As the seals beach themselves on this side, too, they spend a blissful few months devoid of regular human disturbance. But on the off chance there is a sudden cause of noise or movement – a fisherman's boat on the river, for example – the colony is provoked to 'flush out' where all individuals rush down to sea (and safety) all at once. At the Ythan, the sight of hundreds upon hundreds of seals moving down into the water as one body is quite incredible. Like hundreds of awkward uncles on a slip 'n' slide, they hump themselves down the sand bank as quickly as they possibly can before hurling themselves into the water with an almighty crash, sending up more sea spray than a winter storm. The sea then becomes a seething soup of seals swimming out or bobbing along in the estuary mouth. For some reason unknown to us, there came a time of day when our seal colony would, quite suddenly, perform this noisy exercise completely in the absence of any disturbance at all. I can only guess that this was due to the tides; as the tide went out, this possibly signalled feeding time. One seal would decide he was hungry and drive out to the hunting grounds at sea, and the rest would apparently agree in unison.

Seals are naturally inquisitive souls. They are, in fact, very similar in nature to dogs; happily investigating any source of interest, sticking

Our little pea-green boat.

Seals and where to find them

* Beaches, sand bars and rocky outcrops are the best places to spot seals, as they 'haul out' and rest from being out at sea. They can also be found in estuaries and inter-tidal ones, taking advantage of the exposed sand at low tide.

* Notably sizeable colonies in England can be found at Donna Nook in Lincolnshire, Mutton Grove in West Cornwall, and Blakeney point nature reserve in Norfolk. In Scotland, head to the Ythan (obviously) and the Moray Firth.

* If you're feeling particularly adventurous, you can get a chartered boat out to islands just offshore that boast large colonies of seals. Skomer island in Pembrokeshire, the Orkney Islands and the Outer Hebrides are all good places, as well as the Farne Islands in Northumberland. The latter is, for me, the best place to do this, and you can even dive with them.

* You can see seals all year round, but the best times are when they come to land to moult and breed. For greys, this is anywhere between September to January. They raise their pups on land, and as these are white and fluffy they're also very easy to spot.

* For harbour seals, it's June to September. Their pups are slightly more hardy, and are more likely to be in the water.

their noses in every nook and cranny. However, they are happiest to do this when in water where they can move with a rapidity and fluid grace unachievable on land. As if racing you, they will follow you as you walk along the water's edge, disappearing and reappearing at intervals. Some of the most brazen will slip beneath the waves only to pop up a few feet nearer to you for a closer look. Further south, in the sea surrounding the Farne islands, you can go scuba diving to see a seal colony in their natural environment. Look over your shoulder, and a whiskered face stares back at you through your mask, touches your gloved hand with its nose, before flipping over and speeding back through the water.

Boats, too, are a source of amusement. We often headed out with a recreational salmon fisherman on the Ythan, in a little pea-green boat. The seals would come within five feet of the boat, peering up at us, assessing and snorting at intervals. Once our lack of threat had been ascertained, they would flip-turn like Olympic swimmers at the end of a length, and disappear leaving only a few ripples in their wake.

In all my time with seals, I never experienced or saw any aggression, even when meeting one under water. However, their inquisitive nature has got them into trouble. Recreational salmon fishing is a big past-time at the Ythan and therefore conflict has emerged between the angling society and the vast seal population, a topic which was the concern of my dissertation. I spent a lot of time talking with fishermen, who strongly believed the seals were feasting on salmon and posed a threat to anglers in boats. Data on salmon stocks for the Ythan showed salmon numbers were actually on the rise, however many individuals would come very close to the boat, sometimes even swimming underneath. A male grey seal can grow up to 7m in length; it is easy to see why some anglers might be intimidated by a wild animal of substantial size showing a keen (albeit harmless) interest in their distinctly small fishing boat. A cull is forever being proposed but, thankfully, has never been allowed. I believe this is the same case for other parts of the UK. But seals remain (apart from a few exceptions) protected under legislation and I, for one, hope this will never change, and that we continue to find joy in their lazy boy antics for a long time to come.

Seal etiquette ...

Seals may be naturally inquisitive and look like dogs, but remember they are a wild animal (and large at that). Seals can have a nasty bite! Maintain a respectful distance and don't disturb, especially during pupping season when females may feel vulnerable and protective. Also, keep pooches on a lead.

If you find a stranded seal or pup that you suspect to be injured or orphaned, don't attempt to pick it up or get too close as this may stress out the animal. Phone the **RSPCA**, relevant **Wildlife Trust** branch or the **British Diver's Marine Life Rescue** hotline. If it's a pup, try to monitor it for 24 hours – it's not uncommon for mothers to leave their pups for extended periods, and many pups are brought into care unnecessarily because they're mistaken as abandoned. Look out for tell-tale signs – is it thin, weak or lethargic? If the answer is no, then Mum might just be out getting the dinner in.

The sea cliffs of Canna vertigo inducing to say the least.

The Isle of Canna: a bird-watcher's paradise

On the map of Scotland, it looks as though someone has taken a hammer to the west coast and smashed the land into tiny little pieces, which then drifted out to sea and spread about the coastline like dandelion seeds. This smattering of islands form the Inner and Outer Hebrides; weather-beaten, rugged but astoundingly stunning landscapes steeped in culture and tradition. Whilst some presume these exposed islands must be lacking in biodiversity, they are actually some of the best places to experience marine life. They are hotspots for cetaceans and every summer, boats overladen with expectant tourists head out in the hopes of seeing pods of dolphins dancing in the surf or minke whales exhaling plumes of steam. An exceptionally lucky few have even caught glimpse of orcas speeding past, gangs of boisterous predators attracted by the burgeoning populations of seals clustered on the rocky shorelines. The seas here are rich in fish, which also make these islands a haven for seabirds. Sea cliffs are crowded with gabbling colonies of seabirds stuffed into every nook and cranny or filling the skies, wheeling overhead or divebombing into the crashing waves below. All manner of different species colonise anything they can find; even marker buoys are covered in them, clinging on for dear life as they sway violently with the current. A couple of hours on the ferry is a lesson in just how much coastal habitats have to offer.

The Small Isles are an archipelago of islands nestled amongst the Inner Hebrides. They comprise of four main islands; Rum, Muck, Eigg and Canna. Each has its own unique character – Muck is green pastures and rolling hills; Eigg rough and dominated by the rocky outcrop known as An Sgùrr. Rum is the largest and most imposing, with sheer cliffs and formidable peaks that rise dramatically out of the sea. And directly across the sound, peering up at its older brother, lies one of my favourite places in the whole of Britain; the Isle of Canna. I've honestly had some of my most joyous wildlife experiences here, which at first may seem a little unexpected. It's the smallest and westernmost of these islands, remote and battered by the elements, a curious mixture of agricultural land and wind-torn sea-cliffs that from a distance, look almost inhabitable. But looks can be deceiving. Seals lounge languidly in the harbour mouth, whilst the dramatic cliffs are filled with all manner of seabirds occupying any ledge they can find, or tailing fishing boats in great

Razorbills hanging out on a cliff edge.

flocks, settling on patches where the fish have clustered. Further inland, you can stumble across birds you'd be hard pressed to seek out on the mainland. The naturally secretive corncrake sounding its distinctive rasping call from a bed of nettles, or the ghostly shriek of a Manx shearwater in the dead of night. Not to mention it hosts a healthy population of Scotland's 'celebrities'; the white-tailed eagle, our largest bird of prey.

Perhaps the reason that allows wildlife to thrive is the miniscule population – at time of writing, there is a grand total of seventeen people living on the island. This number goes up somewhat during tourist season, when intrepid explorers clomp about clad in hiking boots, but for the most part, Canna's wildlife is left in blissful peace, unless you class the fierce winds and storms that occasionally pop over for a visit. I'm lucky enough to class two of the permanent residents as friends, and I've had many memorable wildlife encounters on this tiny, yet mighty, island.

As the ferry drifts lazily across Canna sound the island comes into view, turning slowly like a jewel on display. On approach, it is hard not to notice the extensive seabird colonies scattered about the coastline, gregarious and delightfully noisy. Leaning over the railings, I often see clusters of cormorants clinging to rocky outcrops, stretching out their wings to dry like dramatic impersonators of Count Dracula, or guillemots divebombing into the waves, fast as bullets. Gulls fly alongside as we sail, riding the currents of the wind. They come in all shapes and sizes; black-headed, herring, little and common gulls, all scanning the waters for tasty shoals of fish.

Once safely disembarked, it's more than worth braving the elements and having a wander around the island's edge. Tiptoeing along the sea cliffs is the very definition of 'blowing away the cobwebs'; the wind tears at the landscape, stirring the sea into a seething mass and whipping my hair into a frenzy so that I come away with that attractive, 'electrocuted' look. Picking my way across the edge, I'll eventually work up enough courage to peer over the precipice and look down at the shrieking, chattering cities of seabirds. It sounds like a hundred hen parties screeching to be heard over one another, and the smell ... well, let's just say there's something fishy about it. That aside, they can be fascinating to watch. In no other place will you find such a diversity of species all in one space, so openly exposed. Lying on your stomach, you can easily while away an hour or two watching the comings and goings, the characters on display and the general soap operas of seabird life.

These colonies truly do live life on the edge. Those sitting calmly on the edge of a sheer cliff face seem so nonchalant about

Guillemots living life on the edge.

Shag in flight.

their position, some nodding off for a snooze, others ruffling their feathers and shifting their weight to a more comfortable position. Clinging onto corners are bands of shags and guillemots with their elegant C-shaped necks, apparently unfazed by the waves crashing beneath them. And, perched on exposed crevices, are razorbills. Looking almost penguin-like in their monochrome uniforms, these birds choose a mate for life and only return to land to breed. I always think they look like a Gentoo penguin's hipster cousin; similar in shape, but with minimalist, geometric markings of two white stripes on a black face, one down the centre of the beak and one between the eyes. Look out to sea, and there will be more birds bobbing about in the waves like corks, or swarming down on fishing vessels in a flurry of wings. Shags, gulls and puffins will be zipping in and out of the caves and crevices, either heading out to hunt or returning to make a hasty crash landing onto the rocks, treacherously slippery with seaweed.

Higher up, fulmars and kittiwakes huddle together like rows of jars on a well-stocked shelf. Kittiwakes, plumped up and brooding, sit on nests that are crammed onto small shelves in the rock, looking either bored or worrisome with their heads buried deep into their bodies to shield against the wind. These ledges are often so narrow that the nest material pokes precariously out over the edge, and I frequently wonder how the chicks don't roll out by mistake. The rock face below is decorated with streaks of white, as though a tin of paint has been spilled. This is where that unpleasant odour emanates from; the scent of weeks' worth of droppings, dried and plastered onto the wall by sun and wind.

Kittiwakes are some of the most characterful to watch. While one parent waits it out with the kids, the other will be out at sea gathering food. Upon the hunter's return, things will become very excited. He often teeters on the edge of the little platform, wings flapping furiously as he attempts to balance whilst delivering his wee offering. How his efforts are received vary with each pair. Sometimes, the recipient is gracious and welcoming, and will rub him affectionately with her beak or huddle in close. Other times, she is nippy and reprimanding, turning her back to him almost as soon as the gift has been delivered I guess these must be the fussier eaters!

If you have a good pair of binoculars, you can peer at the details of these birds and observe the adaptions they have to cope with life at sea. Fulmars, for example, have a curiously shaped beak, dark grey

Kittiwake colony.

or yellow with a rounded, bulbous tip and a 'tube' like structure on the top, which helps to remove salt from the body. They also have a brilliant adaption to ward off predators, spraying a substance made from their own stomach oil out of their beaks which could matt the plumage of their enemy, and prevent them from flight. I've only seen this behaviour once, whilst on Canna, when a Great Skua flew a little too close to a nesting fulmar. Needless to say, it proved a very effective method.

Speaking of Great Skuas, I've had one or two memorable encounters with these birds myself. One day, whilst hiking out to check out Canna's infamous puffin stack (more on this later) I was the unfortunate victim of a Skua attack. Also going by the glorious name of a 'bonxie', they are a canny size – like an exceptionally large gull – and are wicked pirates of the seas, vehemently harassing other, smaller birds to steal their food or even to kill and eat the birds themselves. In summer, bonxies migrate from their wintering grounds in Africa and Spain and flock to the northernmost isles to breed. Their nurseries of choice are coastal, rocky islands, specifically open pastureland – as such, Canna is perfect.

The walk to the stack takes you across open bogs and vast

expanses of overgrown pasture, rippling in the breeze and spattered with bog cotton, their fluffy white seed heads swaying hypnotically. On this occasion, I stumbled in a bog and filled my wellies with oozy, glutinous mud, which meant walking was accompanied by a symphony of squelches. Highland cows eyed me with lazy interest as I scaled rough-stone walls, and the distinctive zinging 'pee-wit' of lapwings heralded my crossing. I'd never seen so many of these beautiful little birds. They crowded overhead, showing off their white bellies and emerald-black plumage, their heads sometimes adorned with an elaborate, curly crest. The lapwing used to be a familiar feature of farmland, but has suffered severe declines over the last ten years due to large-scale changes in agricultural practice. It is now a red listed species, which is incredibly sad – everyone should hear its delightfully bonkers call reverberating around the countryside. To me, it sounds like the bad sound effects of an '80s sci-fi movie.

Past the lapwings and the coos, I was startled by the presence of something enormous lifting up ominously out of the grass. At first, I thought it might be an eagle – it was a big bird, with mid-brown, speckled plumage decorated with white flashes. Its beak was hooked and short, its wings arched as it heaved itself up into the air. At first it seemed to be flying away, but as I shielded my eyes for a better view, it did a swift U-turn and swung back in my direction, right at me in fact. Suddenly it was upon me, feet outstretched, squawking violently, and I threw my arms over my head as I was successfully divebombed. I must have stumbled across the nest of a bonxie. I found out the hard way

An angry bonxie (Great Skua) in full attack mode.

Inside the nest.

– they have zero fear of humans, and will proceed to bombard you until you have left the vicinity. I watched her launch an attack on me of such speed and fearlessness that I couldn't help but be impressed. As I moved through the battle ground, intermittently being swooped upon, I stumbled across the nest: a hollow in the ground, filled with dried grass and around the size of a large serving plate. Inside lay two huge, speckled, greenish-brown eggs, like dull coloured jewels. By this point, Mama was getting extremely haughty (understandably), shrieking and sometimes nearly taking my eye out, so I only stopped for a quick photo before dashing off to leave her in peace. Throughout the day I came across no less than three other angry bonxies, each as livid and fearless as the last.

Puffin.

If there is one animal Canna is famous for, it would be the puffin. Puffins are perhaps the nation's favourite seabird, being delightfully bumbling and comedic. They have a distinctly clownesque appearance: a round, white face with exaggerated cheeks; cartoonish, red-rimmed eyes and bright orange legs that end in over-sized webbed feet. Not to mention its characteristic bill, wedge-shaped and striped in candy colours. It is famed for its endearing personality, sometimes waddling curiously towards unsuspecting tourists during breeding season. Canna is well-known for its 'puffin stack', an enormous flat-

topped rock formation just off the eastern coastline of Sanday that accommodates a huge number of puffins each year. In the spring months, puffins come in to land to breed, digging burrows in soft soil – sometimes even taking advantage of abandoned rabbit holes. It can be a wonderful spectacle, with hundreds of these amazing little birds coming back to the stack from a long day out hunting to roost in their burrows. However, you have to get the timing right. According to local knowledge, 4pm is the golden hour to see them active before they disappear underground. Despite my best efforts, I always seem to have missed this golden window of opportunity . The last time I tried there was no-one home, but instead a great number of little dots in the water that, upon careful squinting, were identified as puffins. Granted, it is a beautiful place to sit; directly across from the striking silhouette of Rum with an extensive colony of kittiwakes to the west. I waited it out for a while, wandering backwards and forwards between the kittiwakes and the stack, where razorbills teased me, appearing suddenly from a crevice and looking more and more puffin-like as the time went on. Eventually, the weather turned. Black clouds threatening rain rolled overhead, and I turned heel and

The famous puffin stack, sadly devoid of any puffins.

went home, admitting defeat as the rain lashed against my back.

The time I finally found puffins, I was on a completely different part of the island. I'd been scoping out golden eagle eyries, following the narrow trail that leads up through the hills and along the very edge of some of the highest cliffs. The golden eagles here are quite unusual; normally, they can be found nesting in trees, great masses of twigs and foliage that hang low in the boughs. But on Canna, the eagles have taken advantage of the relative safety that a sheer rock face can provide. I'd been taken out by a very kind golden eagle expert, who'd been monitoring these eagles for over twenty years. He stationed us in a prime viewing spot, a vertigo-inducing location adjacent to a fantastic row of cliff faces that ballooned out towards the bottom, like bells. He'd set up the telescope on the nest, and we were waiting patiently for any signs of action. This pair were extremely crafty, and had nested in a tunnel carved into the rock face. They seemed to have a very efficient sanitary system. One opening had a mass of nest material protruding out of it, presumably where the chick slept and hunkered down against the wind. The other end was daubed in white, obviously acting as a kind of toilet, keeping unwelcome leavings away from the sleeping and feeding quarters. I had quite amusing images of the chick wriggling backwards to stick its bum out of the second opening, as though it were a medieval peasant aiming for the troughs of sewage below.

We'd seen evidence of eagles in the area and so were quite hopeful that they had nested, and that a chick was snuggled inside. Lying about the fence that bordered the cliff edge was not one, but four golden eagle pellets. These are, essentially, the bits of prey that the eagle can't digest, compressed and compacted into a neat little package that the eagle regurgitates – a behaviour that I think belies its regal image. Tufts of fur, bits of bone, sometimes even feet, are all mixed in together with grass and saliva. The ones we found were still fresh, damp and still intact. Disclaimer: if you are eating whilst reading this book (which I would always encourage, snacks and a hot beverage go hand in hand with books) I would advise you not to look at the following photograph.

However, after three hours there was no further sign of eagle activity. There was just us, the wind rushing through the grass behind our viewing point, and the thunderous crash of the waves below as they slapped against the headland. We kept ourselves entertained by watching the enormous seabird colonies below; the gulls that swarmed about a spindly, finger-like stack, the razorbills that skimmed the surface of the water. And, much to my excitement, puffins! Interspersed between the other birds, they zipped in and out of the

cliffs; little bombardiers that crashed into the sea. The thing I love most about puffins is the way they land; feet first. As they approach a rock, they sail with wings held aloft and those out-of-proportion feet splayed out, like Olympic long-jumpers in orange stockings. Some flew with their mouths stuffed with sandeels, glinting silver when the light caught them. On land, they waddled to and fro, wings folded neatly behind their stocky bodies, or simply stood and observed nothing in particular. And, if you angled your ears right and the wind had died down, in between the waves you could hear them, cooing deeply from the depths of their burrows. It is a rather odd, comical sound; a guttural grunt that sounds almost like a belly-laugh when repeated.

I was so enraptured by these wee comedians that I forgot entirely about the eagle eyrie. Sheepishly, I rose from my stomach, dusted off the grass and returned to my companion at the telescope. He was on the verge (given our position on the cliffs, I mean this both literally and hypothetically) of calling it a day. Not even the slightest stir had come from the nest, and the skies were empty of swooping shadows. We swapped places, he off to see the puffins, me to hold the fort for one last time. Shifting behind the eyepiece, I managed to knock the carefully placed equipment out of place. Cursing my clumsiness, I peered back down through the lens and attempted to readjust it. It was then I spotted a suspiciously eagle-shaped rock at the top of my field of vision. Somehow it looked a different colour to the surrounding landscape; ruddy-brown, with a little white tip. I pulled back from the telescope and shook my head. We'd been out in the field for a good few hours, and sometimes the mind can play tricks on you at this point. I'd learnt this the hard way whilst working in Africa, getting everyone I was guiding excited about a white rhino on the horizon. We watched it for some time, until anxiously I presumed it dead. Thankfully, it turns out there are a lot of rhino shaped rocks in the Savannah ... just as there might be a lot of eagle shaped outcrops on Canna. I looked again, and this time I thought I saw it move – an imperceptible turn of the head. This was getting ridiculous! There was no way we'd been sitting across from a golden eagle for however long, after hours of deeming the nest void. I looked again, and this time it seemed even more eagle like. It was perched like a gargoyle, eerily still except for the pure white head which jerked stiffly from side to side. I called the expert back up to have a look, expecting him to mock my mistake.

'Yep,' He said, squinting through the eyepiece. 'That's an eagle if I ever did see one.'

Maybe my clumsiness isn't so bad after all.

On the CalMac ferry, there is a pencil drawing of the Small Isles, intricately detailed with pictures of their stand-out features and wildlife. Above Canna is a ginormous sea eagle, flying with wings outstretched and eyes glinting with malice. I've been lucky enough to see these incredible wildlife spectacles for myself, and it's certainly something I'll never forget.

Sea eagles have had a tumultuous relationship with humans. They were hunted to extinction in the 1800s, and only recently (in zoological terms) brought back, reintroduced to the west coast in the 1970s. Their return was controversial, largely down to livestock conflicts. Sea eagles are believed by crofters to take lambs, although evidence predominantly suggests they scavenge the weak and feeble that have died naturally; although some specific pairs have been thought to directly predate them, these cases are few. As such, the sea eagle has received a great wealth of media attention, both because of its fearsome reputation and its celebrity-like status as a conservation success story. Over the last few years especially, the population has soared and the west coast is one of the best places to see one.

In fact, if you're in the vicinity, they're quite hard to miss. Our largest bird of prey, and the fourth largest in the world, they have a wingspan of 2.5m and a standing height of almost 1m – this makes them pretty darn conspicuous. The day I saw them, I named 'the day of eagles' – I like to pretend sometimes that my life is some sort of epic, chaptered by suitably epic-sounding adventures. It was the kind of day I'd set out not knowing what I'd find, and coming back with tonnes of stories to tell. I'd literally only just set off, climbing up through a narrow gorge, when something large appeared in my peripheral vision. Immediately I recognised it as a golden eagle; its plumage was rusty brown, the wings fringed with white and extended

into 'fingers' that distinguish the golden eagle's silhouette. It had a broad, fan-shaped tail, and weaved its way up the valley against a backdrop of cornflower blue sky. The golden eagle is perhaps one of Scotland's most iconic animals, all regal magnificence and statuesque beauty. That day, I saw no fewer than six golden eagles at various locations, an astounding number considering on the mainland I'd be incredibly lucky to see just one. I got so used to them, in fact, that I almost shook off something else as 'just being another golden eagle'. But as this one flew right overhead, I suddenly realised my mistake. Firstly, it was ENORMOUS, with great, broad wings, as big as barn doors. Secondly, the head was paler than the rest of the body – a creamy white – and the plumage generally more lighter brown. This was no golden eagle, this was a sea eagle. Its tail confirmed it; wedge shaped and white, which lends it its second name; the 'white-tailed eagle'.

The majestic sea eagle.

I felt my jaw drop at the sight of it. The setting was perfect: I stood on a small ridge on the Tarbert road, which wound its curvy path round the eastern headlands to Sanday, with Rum in the distance and the turquoise waters of the west coast glittering in the sun. I didn't think I'd ever seen something so majestic. There is something about the dramatic, sweeping landscapes of the west coast that so befits the very essence of a bird of prey, especially one so enormous. It was almost as if the sea eagle owned the sky and was surveying its kingdom from a great height, gliding from one corner to the other on great, sweeping wings.

So, there you have it. The Isle of Canna: a bird watcher's paradise, with so much special wildlife to encounter that I could write a whole book on just that.

The Tarbot road, the playground of sea eagles.

Some of the best seabird colonies to visit

Canna is not the only place to catch sight of these amazing birds. Here are some top picks to see these noisy mariners for yourself:

* **Gannets:** Bass rock, Firth of Forth, Scotland. The single largest colony of gannets in the world, with no less than 150,000 individuals! Also keep your eyes peeled for guillemots, razorbills and shags.

* **Kittiwakes and gannets:** Bempton cliffs, East Yorkshire. A managed nature reserve with a huge population of kittiwakes and gannets, as well as razorbills and puffins.

* **Puffins:** Farne islands, Northumberland or South Stack Cliffs, Anglesey are both great places to spot puffins. The latter is an RSPB reserve.

* **Terns:** Forvie sands, Aberdeenshire. Not just famous for seals, this nature reserve is special because of its breeding tern colony, which includes sandwich, common, arctic and the rarer little tern.

Some tips: Generally, the best time of year is summer, between April and August, when the greatest variety of seabirds come to land for the breeding season. Once the last of the young have flown the nest in autumn, many of our cliffs fall silent again. However, we do get migrant species in winter, too, attracted by our food-rich waters; look out for storm petrels and shearwaters.

Catching sight of eagles!

Sea eagles and 'goldies' are part of Scotland's 'big five', and you can only find them North of the border. Luckily, they can be spotted all year round, and are usually very recognisable. Golden eagles have characteristic 'fingers' on the end of their wings, which can be used to distinguish them from the commoner buzzard. Sea eagles are very large, with a bright, white tail and soaring flight.

✻ **Golden eagles** are most likely found skimming the treetops of pine forests, or emerging from rocky ridges at the top of hills. Lofty viewpoints are recommended – the Isle of Harris has a perfectly placed eagle observatory, and Skye has a number of wildlife hides in 'eagle territory'. On the mainland, the Findhorn valley of Inverness-shire and parts of the Cairngorms are good for eagle spotting. The lesser known Loch Morar is also a great place – look out to the islands in the middle of the loch.

✻ **For sea eagles**, the west coast is where you need to head. Skye and the Isle of Mull are probably your best bet, but you might also have luck in Gairloch, Wester Ross or the Argyll forest. They like sheltered lochs as opposed to exposed, and tend to nest in trees.

Golden Eagle.

The big friendly giants

When I was little, whales seemed like a thing of fiction. My brain could not comprehend an animal of such mind-bogglingly huge proportions, giants that roamed the same seas I paddled in and who travelled further than any intrepid sea voyager. Further still, I couldn't understand why most of these enormous beasts – with the exception of the aptly named 'killer' whale (orca) and, to a lesser extent, the sperm whale – were not remotely threatening. Instead they behaved like gigantic sieves, using their bristle like 'teeth' to extract minute marine life from the sea water. This sparked a whole other set of questions in my inquisitive mind. What if the whale had a tooth missing? How could something of such immense size exist on a diet of tiny things? I likened it to me attempting to live off peas. How remarkable it was, I thought, that whales did use their ginormous bulk to rule the seas; if I was them, I would have my pick of what I wanted for dinner.

Of course, I've become a lot wiser and learnt much more about whales since then. But, perhaps a bit naively, it wasn't until my late teens that I realised you could find them off our shores. I'd always associated them with far-off countries, some of which I'd visited. During a family trip to Canada, I'd seen the formidable, streamlined shadows of a pod of orcas gliding underneath our boat in the waters of the Pacific. And whilst travelling in Mozambique I'd followed a group of humpback whales by speed boat, so close you would get showered with water every time one breached. But whales here? In the rainy old British Isles, with its cold, granite waters? Well, yes, as it turns out.

The thing about whales is that they undertake staggeringly lengthy migrations, travelling great distances to eat and breed, and some of these travels bring certain species of whale to us. Pods of orcas have been spotted mainly off the west coast of Scotland, attracted by the resident seal colonies – the pups are the orca's *plat du jour*. Sperm whales – that's Moby Dick to those of you that are familiar – have been sighted a few times back home, off the north-east coast. These animals are the largest toothed predator alive today and are the finest scuba divers of all mammals, being able to hold their breath for up to 90 minutes in order to hunt the giant squid that lurk 3,000m down. Their sightings are few and far between, but all the more special for it. Between May and September, Britain is also frequented by a gentler visitor – the magnificent humpback whale. They pass by on their journey from warm-water breeding grounds in west Africa to the cooler regions off Iceland and Norway, where they travel to feed. More and more humpbacks have been spotted off British shores over the years – a sign, some say, of recovery. Alongside numerous other species of whale, humpbacks were hunted to near extinction by commercial whalers in the nineteenth and early twentieth centuries; chased for their meat, oil and blubber – the thick, fatty material that lies under the skin of most marine mammals. Unbelievably, it wasn't until the 1980s that the International Whaling Commission (IWC) banned commercial whaling in an effort to save the severely depleted whale populations around the world. Sadly, this does still go on in some parts of the globe, but there is evidence to suggest some species are making a comeback. The humpback is one of them.

With this in mind, I was absolutely determined to see one in British waters. They are beautiful creatures; gliding through the water with a grace that belies their enormity. From my experiences in the Indian ocean, I knew how breath-taking it could be to witness them in the wild. The sight of those vast, dark shapes shifting ominously beneath the waves, before a jet of water and air breaks the surface like a miniature geyser. This is followed by a very large, very knobbly, head, the colour of granite. These knobbly bits are in fact enlarged hair follicles, that have been given the weird and wonderful name of 'tubercles' – which (just in case you were in doubt) distinguish it as a humpback. In Mozambique I witnessed five or six individuals, and much like my childhood self, my brain just couldn't compute their existence. In fact, I was so amazed I forgot to be sea sick; unfortunately, having a passion for marine ecology does not automatically bless you with sea legs. Going off the information I had read previously, this pod was most likely in tropical waters for breeding season – hence the number of them. Spotting them on home ground would be a very different experience. Humpbacks do not tend to migrate together, often travelling alone or with an offspring, so I would most likely only catch sight of one. In addition, I am (much to my dismay) boatless. I would have to rely on binoculars and my knowledge of the coastline.

Luckily, one of the best places in the UK to spot migrating humpbacks was right on my doorstep: Aberdeenshire. 2015 had seen an unusually high number of sightings, however I'd been away the entire summer and missed the golden (or rather, grey and barnacled) window of opportunity. So, the following year, I made it my mission to catch sight of one, although, as I have said and will continue to say throughout this book; wildlife spotting is a labour of love. Animals do not just 'present' themselves to you, and, somewhat rudely, only choose to do so when you are least expecting it, and therefore without anything to capture the moment. Countless times during that summer I trudged to various beaches around Aberdeenshire, sometimes accompanied by friends I'd fooled into coming with me; sometimes blessed by sunlight but most of the time joined by gales and intermittent downpours – as is customary during a Scottish summer. I hung around the vast golden sands of Balmedie, where sand dunes stretch for miles and the sea seems endless. I lurked up by the lighthouse near Torry, my logic being that as it was such a popular haunt with bottlenose dolphins, possibly their substantially larger cousins might come to play too. No such luck. Even the dolphins, who are seen so often gambolling about the harbour mouth, seemed to have gone on holiday elsewhere. I tried further up the coast, at Speyside, and spent an enjoyable yet whale-less day crunching across the pebbled beach. On excursions to the West coast – the place for

The golden sands of Balmedie.

amazing wildlife encounters – I kept my eyes peeled, but to no avail. As summer drew to a close, I became resigned to the fact I'd missed the evasive travellers for another year.

It wasn't until September was almost over, when my ambition of seeing a humpback had been packed away for next summer , that my fortunes began to change. It was a bright, autumn day; the kind when the air is so crisp and clear-cut it makes you catch your breath. A friend and I were walking along Newburgh beach – just down from where the seals haul out at the Ythan – with her two beautiful golden retrievers. These dogs were the perfect companions for excursions. Blue was the more adventurous, small and slight, her fur a Marilyn shade of platinum blonde. Let her off the lead and she would give you a coy glance over her shoulder, before shooting off through the dunes with the characteristic sassy wiggle she was known for. It would be some time before she would resurface above the sea of marram grass, give you a cheeky grin, and then high-tail it off again in a cloud of sand. Bruno is a slightly less independent individual, despite being the size of a small bear. Happily, he would trot off, but only to a safe distance. Then he would return and look to each one of us, like a schoolteacher counting heads on a daytrip, and pad softly off again. On the occasion a smell got the better of him, he would follow that for some time, disappearing after his sister. But after a few minutes Bruno would become quite frantic at the realisation he had lost us, and suddenly would come crashing through the dunes, a mass of sandy coloured woollen bulk, and would only calm down after a scratch behind the ears – so relieved that we had not abandoned him. But Bruno was a good explorer in his own way; if we spotted a bird or seal he would wait patiently, tail wagging furiously and his mouth upturned in a wide smile.

That day, the dogs had their fair share to nose at. Jellyfish littered the beach, glittering like jewels in the late morning sun. Around that time of year, an odd phenomenon seems to happen; a great number of jellyfish beach themselves on the tide, becoming solidified and squat in the absence of water. They are, of course, at this point quite dead, but it serves as a fantastic opportunity for a Zoology lesson. This may be a remnant of childhood that refuses to be abated, but I can't resist poking a beached jellyfish with a stick or the tip of my shoe, watching the body ripple gently in response. But look closer, and you can see the intricacies of the animal. To the naked eye, they may look nothing more than a floating plastic bag, but they are amazing feats of natural engineering. A curious cloud like structure comprises the reproductive organs and stomach, and delicate threads make up an early nervous system called a nerve net, which controls

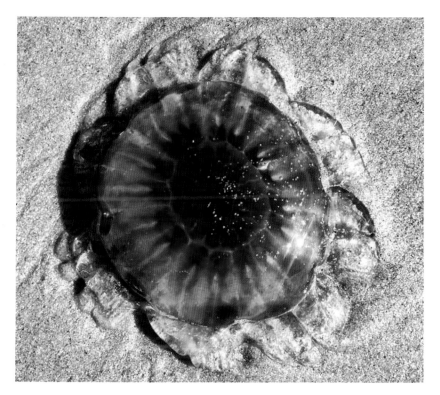

Lion's mane jellyfish washed up on the beach.

movement. Their tentacles are actually armies of specialised stinging cells, called nematocysts, that lie ominously in wait, coiled like springs until some unwitting soul brushes against them. Personally, I feel jellyfish are very pretty to look at, especially when they catch the light. These particular jellies were delicate shades of maroon and magenta, shimmering in rainbow colours where the sunlight reflected. My jellyfish identification skills leave a lot to be desired, but I think these specimens were the lion's mane variety, a cold-water species that carries the impressive title of 'world's largest jelly' – they can grow up to 120 feet long! Their name relates to the extensive strands of stinging tentacles that stream along behind them; a long veil of beautiful weaponry. They have a relatively short lifespan of just one year, and perhaps this is why I see them strewn about the beach every September, like clockwork. The lion's mane used to be relatively uncommon to British waters but more seem to be showing up every year, especially on the North-east coast. They swarm in such great numbers here that fishermen claim to no longer feel their sting, having grown immune from lifting so many out the water. We do have multiple other species that are more common, including my favourite: the moon jellyfish. These delicate little jellies casually float past my mask when I'm scuba diving; almost translucent except for the vivid purple reproductive organs at their core.

Anyway, back to whales. We wandered leisurely up the shoreline, picking our way through the jellyfish corpses and occasionally shouting for Blue, who had disappeared, or throwing a stone for the ever-vigilant Bruno. This was a favourite game of his, despite the fact he wasn't too great at it – for it didn't matter how close into the water we threw the stone, he could never find it again. Bruno would stare and bark expectantly until you gave in and found a suitable rock, before plunging into the surf after it in a more than valiant effort. Still smiling, he would stare into the sea, as if willing it to reappear. Then, he would turn and smile at you as if nothing had happened, and it was you – you wicked, deceitful human – who had not thrown it, and you would have to begin all over again. However, if it weren't for this game, I'd never have seen it.

The first thing that caught my eye was a spout of water shooting up from the horizon. Now, it is slightly unusual to see a jet of water stream skywards out of the sea, and it grabbed my attention. I wondered, at first, if it was a trick of the light; the sun twinkling off the crest of a wave, or catching the windows of a boat. But then it happened again, a little further along the horizon than last time. Excitedly I shouted to my friend, not wanting to take my eyes away. Experience had taught me that attempting to spot things in the sea required immense concentration; the shifting, undulating mass of water confuses things, and you can lose sight of something just by blinking. Shielding our eyes, we stared out to sea. A good few minutes passed, and I began to doubt myself. The spout had been far away on the horizon, a real 'blink-and-you-miss-it' situation. Maybe I had early onset dementia?

Humpback whale breach.

And then, it happened. A gargantuan shape launched itself out of the water, and almost in slow motion turned on its side and landed with an almighty crash. Even from a great distance we got a sense of the sheer size of the animal; the power to be able to hurl itself out of the water, the tidal wave sent rippling out from its landing. The humpack's latin name, *Megaptera novangilae*, literally translates as 'great-wing' - for a reason. As the whale turned, its great pectoral fin – which was almost a third of its entire length – was held

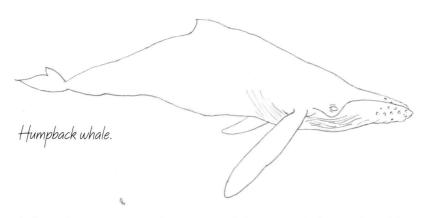

Humpback whale.

aloft, making it appear almost graceful, suspended in mid-air like a ballet dancer. Sometimes, these enormous appendages are slapped off the water's surface, thought to be a method of communication between whales. The breach, however, is the grand finale to a humpback's behavioural repertoire – and it is phenomenal to see. To witness something of such magnificence, of sheer grandeur ... nothing compares, even when you're standing miles away from it. We watched until the brisk chill numbed our fingers, but it seemed our humpback encounter was a brief one. A few blows followed, trailing further out to the horizon. Our whale was carrying on with its journey, just a passing traveller enjoying the ride, pleasantly unaware of its audience on the beach so far away. Putting it down to one of those magical experiences not to be recreated, we called the dogs and followed our footsteps back up the beach, stepping over the jellyfish that were scattered like rubies along the shoreline.

Although finally catching the rare sight of a migrating humpback is hugely rewarding, we have our own native species to appreciate. Whales and dolphins – or 'cetaceans' to give them their posh title – are actually quite a common occurrence. On a field trip in my second year, we stayed in a converted farmhouse on the outskirts of the small town of Cromarty; a jumble of white-washed cottages overlooking the Moray Firth. Being fresh faced zoologists, we hopped onto our RIB with all the enthusiasm and naivety of students promised pods upon pods of dolphins, spinning and jumping about the boat as the sun sparkled off the water and we laughed merrily as the career we had dreamed about was realised. In reality, we set off into skies greyer than the Granite City we had left behind and waters so choppy we couldn't have spotted a dolphin if we'd wanted to. As our boat bounced and slapped through the sea and the driving rain stung our faces, there was not a dolphin to be seen. Although we did see them the following day, as our coach pulled away from the car park, gambolling about in the calmest sea I had ever seen.

I have had much better experiences in the Moray firth since

then. The area is one of those magical places where it seems the conditions are just right for wildlife, and it is rich in an abundance of species and habitats. The firth is particularly famous for its marine life, and it was here I spent some time with another type of whale – the minke. Minke whales are in fact native to Britain, and – luckily for us – are the most abundant of all the baleen whales. 'Baleen' is the name given to whales that have plates of hair-like structures for teeth, that act as filters to catch all the little critters. My master's project considered their movements and habitat use in the Moray firth (essentially, where they were hanging out and why) and, much like the seals, I came to love these little whales with their curious habits. I guess studying something in such minute detail for a year will leave you with an innate fondness and fascination of that thing. I have met people who are enthralled by moss, or loved statistics so much that they dedicate their lives to solving other people's statistical woes; I will never understand this rare breed of person, but I am forever grateful to their presence, being unblessed in the computer coding department. For me, I find minkes so incredibly endearing. Growing to a maximum of 10m in length they are relatively wee – comparatively speaking, when you consider their blue whale cousins of almost 30m. They have the adorable nickname of 'little piked whale' on account of their narrow, pointed snout, and have a slightly grumpy, indifferent expression.

Every time we set out to see minkes it was always a good day, even if the weather didn't behave. We utilised that golden window of opportunity between May and September, which, as a general rule, is the best time to see cetaceans. A tip to spot whales and dolphins is to look for an aggregation of seabirds bobbing around on the waves, otherwise known as a 'feeding frenzy'. The birds will be feasting on a shoal of fish beneath, and other animals will usually follow suit. Sure

Minke whale.

enough, having found a gaggle of gulls or gannets, we would see a couple of small dorsal fins emerge from the water shortly afterward. A minke dorsal fin is easily identifiable, being heavily curved. They are substantially less showy than humpbacks. Although breaches have been reported by some, minkes demonstrate a more laid-back attitude, and mostly it is just their deep grey back you see exposed, just above the water. Before embarking on a dive, they arch their backs extensively, but their tail fluke never breaks the surface – tail slapping is again reserved for their larger, more flamboyant relatives. Instead, they simply vanish beneath the surface, re-emerging a little while later with a gentle sigh.

The minkes we encountered in the firth seemed rather curious of our boat, coming close enough that we could hear their distinctive breathing pattern, which is typically five to six times a minute. Like all baleens, they have two blowholes on the upper part of the head; if they raised their head above the water we could easily count them at this distance. Also noticeable was their brilliant white underside – a stark contrast from the dark back – and a series of grooves that ran down the length of their throat, which enable it to expand hugely during feeding (a capability I would love to have myself). This inquisitive side to the minkes was another thing I loved about them. Lifting their head just out of the water, they would literally spy on us intruders, their elongated noses pointing skywards. Rather fittingly this behaviour is called 'spy hopping'.

On one occasion, I was even more lucky to be able to listen to them. The research vessel was equipped with an acoustic device that allowed us to hear sounds beneath the water, and at the right setting we could nosey in on minke chat. The sea is a vast place, which must be rather annoying should you like to talk to someone – so whales are extremely loud. Minkes make sounds that are approximately 152 decibels: that's like standing next to a plane during take-off. Fortunately, above the surface it wasn't loud enough to burst our eardrums, and we spent a lovely half an hour just listening to them natter away. For a few minutes, there would be nothing but still silence ... and then, a curious series of grunt-like sounds or thumps, which is the language of the common minke. I felt like a small child hiding on the staircase, listening into a forbidden conversation; mischievous, and a little enthralled. It was like being allowed into a secret world. The sounds seemed so other-wordly, these repetitive, tinny pulses that somehow meant something to other whales. While writing up my project, I often thought of those sounds, echoing around the small, stuffy cabin of a boat in the North Sea.

Cardigan Bay coastal pa[th]

Whale and dolphin hotspots

* **Bottlenose dolphins**: The biggest populations in the UK are found in Cardigan Bay, on the west coast of Wales, and the Moray and Cromaty firths in the North of Scotland. Cardigan bay, I've heard on good authority, is brilliant for sightings and was assigned as a Special Area of Conservation (SAC) because of its huge population, which is the biggest in Britain. Smaller numbers can be found regularly in the Shannon estuary on the west coast of island, and numerous places in the Hebrides including Arsaig, Skye and Islay.

* **Minke whales** are very widely distributed, so you have a great chance of spotting one. Catch sight of them all round the Scottish coast, and throughout the North Sea as far south as Yorkshire.

* **Humpbacks** are being sighted more often as they pass by on their migratory routes. The most frequent sightings have come from Aberdeenshire, Norfolk and the Shetland Isles.
  Don't forget to look out for harbour porpoise – our smallest and most familiar marine mammal. They like to hang out closer to shore, in harbours or riverine estuaries. Its blunt, triangular dorsal fin is often confused with those of bottlenose, but a porpoise's is smaller and less curved.

A few tips…The ideal time to see cetaceans is June, when the weather is good and food is plentiful. Generally though, they're about from May to September. Pick a clear day with good spotting conditions, when the sea is calm and the swell low. Look out for seabirds swarming a particular spot, as that should tell you where the fish have aggregated. Dolphins also like to chase the surf made by fast moving boats, as I found out when training to drive our dive club's RIB!

A duel on the dunes

I ronically, most of my favourite encounters with wildlife have occurred at times when I've left the house without my camera. You would think that years of cursing my own stupidity would mean I ensured it was with me on successive outings – sadly, not so. I have the unfortunate combination of an innate childlike desire to be free from cumbersome but useful objects when exploring and the concentration span of a pea, meaning that often my camera and phone remain exactly in the place that I intended to pick them up at the front door. However, in a world where we are constantly obsessed with 'capturing the moment' and sharing it with as many audiences as possible, forgetting such items can actually be a blessing in disguise. I wonder if these experiences have been the best because I am fully 'there'; the experience is not filtered through a lens. They are moments that have taken me completely by surprise, often with such rapidity I could do nothing more than sit there and fully enjoy the spectacle as it unfolded before me.

One such moment happened on a long bike ride whilst at home in Whitley Bay. I had come home on the pretence of writing my first PhD chapter, but as every student will be able to relate to, I ended up doing everything but. There is something so deliciously enticing about a bicycle when you have something else to be getting on with; it promises freedom, a fast track to adventures waiting to be had without any major expense or equipment (apart from, perhaps, the bike itself, which is an integral part). It also just so happened to be my favourite time of year: autumn. The day had that ideal crisp-cut cleanness that only this season can deliver, with cool winter knocking at the front door and the sunny days of summer making a hasty retreat out the back. To me, autumn is the ideal time for wildlife spotting; the muggy air of summer is too oppressive to enjoy it properly, whereas September and October still have the sun and some warmth, but there is more of a clarity that fine tunes the senses. Late Summer and early autumn are the best times to find butterflies, birds and a whole number of other beasties as they prepare for the harsher times ahead. I like to think that the leaves turn colour almost to provide the world with one final siesta before the dark depths of winter set in, falling as confetti when the season ends.

Once upon a time, Newcastle was famous for its vast coal mining industry and its landscape was criss-crossed with tracks for the wagons

The colours of autumn.

that carted this precious resource from the pits. Now they have been turned into paths and cycle tracks through the countryside, and are some of my favourite places to explore. Bordered by hedgerows and surrounded by fields and meadows, they are ideal areas to watch the seasons turn. Berries begin to appear in the foliage, and ripen into vivid Christmas baubles of crimson and burgundy; the leaves turn golden and burnt orange, fluttering down to form a carpet on the dirt track, rising into a flurry when disturbed. Small garden birds – tits of every shape and size, blackbirds, robins and wrens – flit between the trees, calling to each other in chirruping voices. One such path takes you right through from Monkseaton to the coast, changing scenery from lush woods to gorse bushes with their yellow clusters of flower. It leads you to the coastal path by Blyth beach, which winds its way through the sand dunes that undulate on either side.

They may not appear it at first, but dune systems are some of the most ecologically important habitats we have. They are complex ecosystems, built through a long, slow process. The tearing winds that we normally button up our coats against cause the sand to build up and become trapped by specialised plants, such as marram grass. This is the tall, hardened grass that forms carpets across the sand, and spikes your legs no matter what you're wearing. There are few species that can brave the exposed conditions of the tallest dune peaks; they are hardy, resilient plants, resistant to salt and clinging onto the sand with outstanding tenacity. Essentially, they are the foundations of these enormous natural constructions and without them, the dune wouldn't exist. The grasses bind together the grains of sand and stabilise the dune, allowing it to grow in size and for other plants to colonise. But with every peak comes a trough. Erosion of other parts form wetter, more sheltered hollows – or 'slacks' – where a more diverse range of plants can thrive. And, as the dunes stabilise further, they become enriched by decaying plant matter,

An extensive dune system.

encouraging the growth of small shrubs and even wildflowers.

It is this range of conditions – the variation in acidity, exposure, water content – that makes dune systems a surprising place to find wildlife. Many of them are Sites of Special Scientific Interest (SSSI) or Special Areas of Conservation (SAC) because so much of the animal and plant life is rare, perfectly adapted to such a difficult place to live. For example, in some places you can catch sight of sand lizards – one of our rarest reptiles – who bask on exposed patches of sand and even lay their eggs in it. The males can be an eye-popping lime green, with a distinctive brown stripe running along the spine. Many nationally scarce invertebrates reside in the damper depressions, such as the northern dune tiger beetle with his camouflage garb, who parades about the sand on stilted legs like a tiny army officer. Or the delicate, pale 'bright wave' moth, an extremely rare sight fluttering about on fringed wings. Beautiful orchids in shades of mauve, lilac and fuchsia cluster about the slacks alongside foxgloves and wild roses, attracting a host of pollinators, and shelducks nest shyly beneath the gorse bushes. The plants that reside here are heralded by the best names: sea spurge, sea-buckthorn, crowberry, fescue grass, viper's bugloss ... names that satisfyingly tumble off the tongue. There is also birds foot trefoil – named for the curious shape of its leaves – and sea holly, which look like the thistle's classier cousin. Of course, there are seabirds; gulls, terns and waders. Going back to my time at the Ythan estuary, we were once taken to the 'forbidden' side of the reserve to see the tern colonies during their breeding season. Our guide was the wonderful ranger, who took us on a wild 4x4 rollercoaster ride over the dunes, sending up plumes of powdery-soft sand in our wake. Not wanting to disturb the colony, we left the car a good distance away and hiked the rest of the way, breathing in the salt air and revelling in the precious feeling of being the only people there. It was like stepping on freshly laid snow for

Wildflowers growing in the slack.

The tern colony flying above the dunes at Forvie Sands.

the very first time, knowing your footprints will be the first.

Forty minutes later, we were richly rewarded by the spectacular sight of thousands of birds swarming the air like a plague of locusts. The colony is home to all four species of tern: sandwich; common; arctic; and the rare little tern, and it is an internationally important site. Crouched well out of sight, we watched as they wheeled about the skies, some returning from the estuary with a fish clutched carefully in their beak, calling out to the young in the nest. A common tern has a few calls, including a gentle 'kip-kip' sound and a longer, harsher 'kee-arrr'. They were certainly a noisy bunch; it was like listening to an experimental orchestra.

Certainly, dune systems have a plethora of wildlife that belies their tough exterior. But it was a rather unexpected encounter with a raptor that took me by surprise that autumn day in Blyth, as I had a little rest in the shelter of two tall dunes.

Contemplating the sea, three birds caught my eye. They seemed locked in a furious but very acrobatic battle, two of them repeatedly dive bombing a third. I recognised them as ravens, which often moved over from the adjacent farmers' fields. They must have had some sort of treasure hidden amongst the shrubs that was under threat and were vociferously attacking their intruder, uttering harsh guttural cries as they carried out their air strike. For a moment, they abated and I could identify the third – a sparrowhawk. One of the smaller raptor species, they have an amazing ability to hover in the same spot with surprising accuracy, as though suspended from string. They often perform this behaviour over fields or long grass, where they seek out potential meals with incredibly powerful senses.

I'd seen sparrowhawks many times before; they are quite common in Northumberland, especially in the countryside. But never had I seen it so close, and in such an impressive aerial battle. For at least five minutes, the raven pair courageously warned off their unwelcome visitor, and the three birds pirouetted, wheeled and swooped at great speeds as if performing a complex dance. Intermittently (and rather cheekily, I thought) the sparrowhawk would attempt to hover again, with that odd stillness that made it appear to be flying against some invisible wall. At one point, the hawk hovered right above my head, quite low so that I was able to see all of its features; the delicate yet sharp curve of its beak, the beady black eyes, the white underside flecked with pale brown. A powerful predator in miniature, its daintiness belies the serious abilities within. I watched it dive, plummeting from its hover with astonishing precision to capture the prey my own mediocre eyes could not detect, whilst the ravens cried their angry indignation.

After that, the sparrowhawk vanished amidst the scrub, and the ravens lost interest. I waited for another few minutes, but guessed the hawk must be polishing off its meal and decided to leave it undisturbed, thinking I'd already had enough luck to witness a hunt in full action, complete with pre-dinner entertainment. But moments after setting off on my bike, I noticed the sparrowhawk again. I stopped; it hovered, suspended in motion. I continued, and it flew along beside me, swooping and diving as it went. This individual must have been particularly wanted in these parts, because as we moved on together it also was chased off by no less than two common gulls and another pair of ravens. Eventually, like a weary, misunderstood gunslinger in a bad Western, the hawk veered off and disappeared into the sunset.

Some dune systems worth visiting

* **Bridgend, Glamorgan, South Wales:** Known as the 'welsh Sahara', Europe's second biggest dune system stands at a staggering 800 acres. Explore the Merthyr Mawr nature reserve, or surf down the dunes largest peak, 'the big dipper'.
* **Braunton Burrows, Devon:** if it's international importance you're after, look no further than this UNESCO biosphere site – appointed on account of its incredible diversity of wildflowers. Sefton Coast, Merseyside: with 22 miles of beaches to wander, keep your eyes peeled for natterjack toads and sand lizards
* **Sandwood Bay, Sutherland:** For the more adventurous. A four-mile hike from the nearest single-track road, experience the peace and quiet of these dunes and the breath-taking views of the Buachaille sea stack.

FRESHWATER

To quote Disney's Pocahontas: 'you can't step in the same river twice'. This is exactly why I love them – one river is never the same from one day to the next. They are constantly evolving and changing. An idyllic, placid scene one day might become a seething, frothing mass the next, threatening to burst its banks.

And of course, a river varies so much geographically. It begins high up in the mountains as a ferocious beast, rushing over rocks and pounding through valleys at a furious pace. As the altitude lessens and the land flattens out, the river calms slightly, carving meanders out of the landscape and leaving steep banks and overhangs in its wake. As it slows, its course straightens out and becomes an area of serenity so far removed from its fast-paced earlier life, allowing thick reed beds and luscious vegetation to grow, interspersed with sandy banks and pebbled shores. All this variation brings with it a rich diversity of wildlife, from the salmon and trout that struggle their way against the icy rapids, to the insects that dance across the water's surface and the multitude of birds and mammals that feed on them. Sand martins and water voles nest in the banks. Ducks float along with the current and invert themselves every so often to feed, bums and legs left sticking out of the water like little synchronised swimmers. Herons inch their way along the shallows, scrutinising the water beneath, whilst dragon- and damsel-flies zig-zag across the surface, their vibrancy catching the eye. If you're lucky you might catch sight of a kingfisher perched regally on a submerged log, or even an otter scrambling about amongst the grass and boulders.

But it isn't just rivers that can be rewarding places to spot wildlife. Our lakes and ponds are also teeming with things to see, including swallows that perform beautiful aerial displays alongside a whole host of weird and wonderful insects. There are freshwater shrimp, aquatic snails and my favourite, the water boatmen, who seemingly 'row' themselves across the water on needle-thin oars. These are prime places to see amphibians – frogs, toads and newts – most of whom are an endangered species nowadays, being particularly vulnerable to climate change. Seeing frogspawn, a little white cluster of jelly orbs floating on the surface, always evokes memories of childhood, of waiting for the little tadpoles to hatch and watching

their fascinating transformation into adult form. It still excites me a little, and I have to suppress the urge to scoop some up into a tub to take home. And, especially in the North of the country, we have the Big Guns: birds of prey. Some species, such as ospreys, feed off the bounty of fish offered by our freshwater habitats and can be seen crashing dramatically into the water, talons extended, to grab their fish takeaway. Some even nest in the surrounding area, and if you are incredibly fortunate you might be able to follow the chick's progress from hatching to an awkward fledgling, balancing precariously on the edge of the nest.

However, one of the best things about freshwater is that it's normally pretty accessible. Most parks or gardens will have a pond; peer in and see the pond skaters skimming the surface, or the tiny fish darting to and fro. Monitor frogspawn (a particularly great thing to do with kids – my niece adores it), or search for newts amongst the reeds. If there isn't a river near, there is bound to be a tiny tributary stream bumbling along that joins to it. These have the added bonus of often running through woodland, or the hedgerows at the base of a field, and as such are the ideal places to find little garden birds. And it doesn't even have to be a permanent feature. An area of a field that has become flooded after heavy rain will become deliciously marshy and boggy, and may even turn into a wetland habitat that attracts wading birds and even some migratory visitors, as I discovered not too far from where I live. It can even make you feel a little better about our soggy climate ... well, sometimes.

Be it the wilderness of a river; a tiny babbling stream, a serene pond or even a temporary marshland, there is a whole wealth of wildlife to discover in these habitats. Just make sure you wear wellies.

Grey Heron.

The Montrose basin

his chapter begins where a river ends; at an estuary. I struggled with where to fit this story – it classes both as coastal and freshwater. But it bridges the gap nicely between sea and river; just as in real life, one flows into the other.

Estuaries are some of the best places to spot wildlife. The place where a river ends its journey, widening out to meet the sea, can be an odd, mixed-up environment and as such supports a suitably mixed-up jumble of creatures. Brackish water – the name given to the cocktail of fresh and saltwater as it mixes – can be a challenging environment to live in. Conditions change hourly; the tides influence the amount of saltwater and thus the chemical composition of the area, switching between high and low salinity. But all this variety creates a rich diversity of habitats. Sandbanks rise up near the estuary mouth piled high with marram grass; thick walls of reeds stand tall at the river's edge, and salt marshes stretch on for miles with their furry clumps of salt-tolerant plants. And, when the tide has rushed out, mud flats are left behind, vast expanses of delightfully sticky, oozy mud that have claimed more than a few unfortunate wellies.

This diverse assortment of habitats make estuaries some of the most productive ecosystems on the planet. The tall grasses and reeds are perfect hidey-holes for nesting birds and small mammals, and the sandbanks provide refuge for seals in need of a nap. Sea birds and shorebirds, such as curlews and sandpipers, pick their way along the water's edge, pecking at the myriad tiny beasties that live in the silt. Otters and ducks may drift casually with the current at high tide, and, once the water recedes, the exposed mudflats become a banquet for wading birds like redshanks, oystercatchers and sanderling, who enjoy the feast of invertebrates that thrive in the gooey layer of mud beneath them. In fact, these minute creatures are at the heart of an estuarine ecosystem, providing an abundance of food for birds and marine life, and in turn, the predators that feast on these. Estuaries can be a cornucopia of wildlife, and a day spent spotting can be incredibly rewarding.

One of the most successful days I've ever had in the UK – in terms of the sheer amount of animal encounters – was at a place called the Montrose basin. The basin is the tidal estuary of the river South Esk and is surrounded by an enormous local nature reserve that incorporates a plethora of habitats. Saltmarshes, freshwater streams, extensive reed beds, arable land bordered by hedgerows, and vast, squelchy mud flats that hide a multitude of miniature super-creatures who support the rich diversity of life that can be found there. Upon first look, the mud looks entirely unremarkable; a dull, greyish-brown colour, covered in tiny holes and giving off odd sucking sounds every now and again. At best, it glistens slightly in the sunshine. But it also houses thousands of invertebrates, from miniscule marine snails called Hydrobia, to Corophium – tiny shrimp-like creatures that build little tubes out of sand. Most important of all to the basin are lugworm, easily found by the funny little piles of mud they leave behind when excavating their burrows. Essentially, as the worm chomps its way down through the silty sand, whatever goes in just comes straight back out the other end. This gives it the rather attractive name of 'pseudo-faeces' – it's not actually poop, but the remnant of a messy renovation.

This abundance of invertebrate life attracts a great number of shorebirds and waders. Curlews, redshanks and oystercatcher busy themselves pecking at the shoreline, whilst widgeons, shelducks and eider ducks bob along at high tide. I have always had a soft spot for the latter. Their call sounds a bit like a rather portly builder cat-calling a passing woman, and has to be one of my favourite bird calls of all time. The course of the river can also bring with it species from upstream. A grey heron stalked the water's edge on long, spindly legs, squinting into the water at his feet. Herons remind me sometimes of elderly gentlemen; every step carefully placed, shoulders hunched

A kingfisher perched on a log. Taken early in the morning, just as it began to get light.

and neck hung low, to give a stooped appearance. Their plumage is a sleek pale grey, and with wings folded it gives the impression of a long overcoat. A smooth, black comb-over on top of the head and a thin, pale face complete the illusion. I watched the heron make his leisurely way through the shallows, before stretching out deceivingly broad wings and taking flight. There is something a little prehistoric about a flying heron. Their wings are enormous, and they take great, swooping flaps with them held in an awkward angular position. Those lengthy legs are not tucked in, but hang free, nearly dangling in the water beneath.

One of the most surprising sightings of the day was of another river species, although one much smaller and far less common to see. I had been told of the fabled Montrose kingfisher who frequented the patch outside the visitor centre, and was extremely keen to catch sight of it having always wanted to see one in the wild. However, I was cynical. Spotting a specific species is a finnicky business. You can be the most organised and informed person in the world, fully equipped with binoculars in hand, in the exact spot at the exact time ... and the animal you're looking for just won't appear. You wait for hours, only to trek back cold and miserable and find an excited gaggle of walkers in the car park, talking animatedly about their 'unexpected sighting' of a kingfisher.

'Never seen one there before, only today! And I've never seen them do somersaults off the back of an otter, have you? Amazing!'

This seems to happen most often when you want to try your hand at a little photography – animals appear to have an innate sense of when a camera is present, and disappear off the face of the earth. Most of my best and most exciting sightings occur when I'm completely unprepared, and leave me torn between ecstasy at the experience and exasperation at my own stupidity for leaving the house without my camera. I was fully prepared to wait patiently and watch for a flash of blue. Yet, at the basin, luck was on my side. As soon as I arrived, there was the kingfisher, conspicuous in his vibrant uniform of turquoise and burnt orange. He was perched on his 'favourite' log, situated in a small, murky pond on the banks of the estuary, and stood out all the more for his bleak surroundings. Vivid white markings on the side of his head and beak glinted as he turned his head. Kindly, he stayed for long enough for me to snap a few photographs (yes, I had arrived prepared for once) before flitting off through the reeds to attend to more important business than posing. Kingfishers prefer slow-moving or still water, where they can easily detect fish from their perches on the riverside. You're most likely to see one sitting on a log or overhanging branch – like the one at Montrose – but they also can be seen rocketing across the water, hovering every now and again inches from the surface.

I set off on my walk around the basin cheered from the Kingfisher sighting, half expecting my luck to have run out. How wrong I was...

The route around the reserve takes you around the water's edge; past the historic salt pans that were once used to evaporate salt water, leaving behind the thick white crystals, but now are the favourite haunts of wading birds who enjoy the shallow water pools that remain. As I walked past two dunlins, with mottled brown plumage and jet black beaks, pottered about on the marshy ground. On the other side of me stretched the estuary itself. At high tide, seabirds skimmed the surface of the water – the more common herring gulls, but also black-headed and greater black-backed gulls. Their smaller, more delicate cousins – terns – swept in between, crying out in voices that famously sound like squeaky door hinges.

The path took me through farmers' fields to another important habitat; the reed beds. A great, rippling, golden sea of rushes, the reed beds provide vital hiding places for nesting birds. Although they didn't reveal themselves to me, a pair of bearded tits had been spotted here, and it was greatly hoped that they would nest at the site. I did manage to catch a glimpse of a sedge warbler – a small, plump bird that looks similar to many garden birds – hopping between the golden stalks. In the summer months, this habitat would become

a hive of activity, with butterflies dancing above and small birds flitting in and out, carrying parcels of food for little ones or materials with which to build nests.

I wandered down the path with the reeds to my right, in stark contrast to the agricultural land on the other. The farmers here are open to conservation initiatives, and have allowed the boundaries of their land to become overgrown. The corners of these fields held small patches of wildflowers, tumbling over one another in a gloriously messy riot of colour. Measures like this are incredibly important, providing refuge for wildlife and acting as 'corridors', enabling safe passage through otherwise heavily managed land. That is not to say the creatures at the basin did not make use of the farmers' fields. Great Whooper swans settled on the crops, snowy white except for the black mask across their eyes, like bandits. This may sound harmless, but swans can do a fair bit of damage – more than sheep, in fact. Not only do they see the neat rows of seedlings as a convenient banquet laid out just for them, but they also rip up the vegetation with those huge webbed feet. As such, the nature reserve's management has created the country's most intriguing job title; there is a 'swan-scarer' employed with the sole purpose of creating imaginative ways in which to deter hungry Whoopers.

It was on these fields that I had another encounter with something I'd been dying to witness in the wild; hares. They are a prominent feature of Britain's natural heritage; immortalised as much-loved characters in children's books and cartoons. But for 24 years, they had evaded me. I'd seen rabbits – tonnes and tonnes of rabbits – but hares are quite different. They share the same sandy brown fur with accents of white, but a few subtle nuances separate them. Firstly, hares are much larger and tend to sit upright. Their features are generally elongated; the ears are taller and tipped with black, and their face is longer and thinner. The hind legs, too, are also much lengthier and thus more powerful than those of rabbits. They are the Ferraris of the rodent world, using their long stride to cover ground at high speeds with minimal effort.

They are also famous for 'boxing', a behaviour normally seen during the mating season. It is commonplace for the males of many species to compete during these times, engaging in combat or some other kind of display to demonstrate their prowess and impress a female. But with brown hares, it has a much more comical purpose. When a female, or 'doe', grows tired and unimpressed of a buck's advances, she'll whip around and box him away (ladies, take note). However, my trip to the basin was well before mating season even started (usually around March and April), so when I spotted two hares sitting on the field opposite, I didn't expect them to start.

At first, it was quite the stand-off. Ears pricked, fur bristling, they surveyed each other like the sheriff and the out-of-towner from an

A brown hare taking a snooze.

Brown hares 'boxing' and chasing one another.

old Western. For some time, neither moved an inch as they squared one another up; rapidly assessing size, brute strength and the likelihood of a quick getaway. Then, suddenly, the pair sprang into action. Rising up onto their haunches, they pulled their forearms into their body and began to 'box', jabbing at each other and hopping to and fro on their hind legs. It was a furious match – the opponents keeping their heads held back to avoid a blow to the face, giving the impression that they were almost looking down on each other with contempt. For a time, they danced about the field, lunging and parrying drunkenly like a pair of egotistical geezers outside a pub, swaying with the effort of staying upright. Their jabs were ill-placed – there was never any contact, and as far as I could tell no-one was winning.

A few minutes later, the fight was over. The hares sat still for a minute, as if digesting the events that had just unfurled. Then they turned heel and sprinted off across the field, vanishing into the undergrowth at the other side. Seemingly, whatever differences they had had been settled quickly. With the mating season still a few months away, I could only guess that these were immature hares and the boxing match was more of a play-fight in preparation for the real deal. This isn't an unlikely proposal; many youngsters hone their skills at home, with their brothers and sisters. Young stags with small, velvet-soft antlers butt heads in anticipation of a future rutting season on the battlefield, and fox cubs scramble and scrap outside their dens, refining the skills they will need as grown-ups. Play-fight or no, it was a joy to watch and yet another experience to add to the list of my day at Montrose.

Estuaries have their fair share of native wildlife that set up home all year round. But they are also incredibly important for migratory species, who take advantage of the rich bounty of food to refuel, during their often vast travels from other countries. Essentially, Britain's estuaries are the natural world's equivalent of service stations; places to recharge the batteries, have a rest and fill the stomach. Although I am still yet to see a bird downing coffee.

Thousands of summer and winter visitors land on our estuaries every year. Red knots undertake mammoth pilgrimages that belie their tiny size. Widegon – who contrary to their name are in actually a species of duck – arrive from Iceland in early autumn, easily distinguishable with a maroon head and golden crest. But the bird which arrives in the greatest numbers, and certainly with the most amount of noise, is the goose. At the basin, pink-footed geese descend on the mudflats in their droves around September, honking incessantly like a convention of vintage cars. Numbers reach over 80,000 individuals, which, when you think about it, is an astounding amount of one animal. As such, it's an incredible sight.

I've been to the basin a few times just to see the geese return. On a clear day, the late summer sunsets provide the perfect backdrop to watch them fly in from breeding grounds in Greenland, Svalbard and Iceland, to roost overnight. Hundreds of black shapes, silhouetted against skies filled with grapefruit pink, deep orange and pale gold, streaked with dusky purple and baby blue. 'Skeins' – the name given to the characteristic 'v' formation in which they fly – fill the sky, as do the harsh honking calls that they sound to herald their arrival, not unlike the sound of the old-fashioned circus performances involving a sea lion and a set of bulb horns. Once settled, they become a bustling mass of pale grey accompanied by a wall of bright pink feet, gossiping incessantly with one another. At first light, the geese take off again to feed. A penchant for carbohydrate-rich foods such as cereals and grains takes them to arable land, where they arrive in their thousands. The current advice to farmers to prevent decimation of their fields from a goose invasion includes leaving harvested crops for them to feed on.

Our estuaries are becoming ever more important. Climate change and a loss of suitable stopping grounds is seriously affecting migrating birds – without frequent stopping points, it's like running an ultra-marathon without breakfast. Birds are having to travel further to get food and replenish their energy stocks, and more than ever before don't make it to their final destination. Furthermore, the important environmental cues that signal to the birds it's time to take-off, like temperature, are changing. This throws the internal calendars of these species off course, causing them to arrive or leave at the wrong times. This means the food they usually eat may not be there, or physically they may not be fully 'ready' to leave. It is therefore vital our estuaries remain protected, and that we appreciate how biodiverse they actually are; that what appears as a barren land of glutinous mud actually harbours some of the most important mini-beasts, and a pile of sand dunes and salt-marsh can actually be a haven for birds. And they have the added bonus of having something to spot, all year round. So get to your nearest one, and get exploring!

Exe estuary, Devon.

Some of the best estuaries and mudflats ...

* **The Ythan estuary**, half an hour's drive North of Aberdeen, famous for its tern roosts and seal colonies (I'm a bit bias towards this one!)
* **Loch Gruinart, Islay, West Scotland** – a fantastic place to see barnacle geese during the winter, and a huge diversity of wading birds
* **Dee estuary, north Wales** – one of the most important wetland sites in the UK with extensive cockle beds that attract thousands of birds every year
* **Severn estuary, South England** – One of the largest estuaries in Europe, and a designated SAC for its mudflats, lagoons and pastures
* **Exe estuary, Devon** – also known as the 'English Riviera', this is a favourite haunt of the eponymous avocet, the star of RSPB's logo.

What to take with you…warm layers (it'll get nippier as you move towards the sea), waterproof shoes, a good pair of binoculars (or, a long camera lens also does the trick. My binoculars died thanks to the Madagascan humidity, so I've tried and tested this method), and a camera – you never know what you might find.

The otter family

For the past seven years, I've walked along the river Don almost every single day. The river begins its course high up in the Grampians, flowing eastwards through Alford, Kemnay and Inverurie before reaching Aberdeen. Here it runs along the north side of the city; carving a path from Dyce to Old Aberdeen, where it widens and spills into the North Sea. I am fortunate enough that part of it forms my walk to university, and has done since I was a bright eyed, bushy-tailed fresher all those years ago. My daily commute consists of a series of paths that wind their way through Donmouth local nature reserve, of which the Don is a central feature, and I have got to know the wildlife extremely well. The sheer amount of it has always amazed me; given the close proximity to the city and the amount of people that cross the reserve, it's hard to imagine any animal would hang about for long. Yet the park is alive with birds – goldfinch, bullfinch, bluetits and thrush flit from branch to branch, whilst a huge variety of ducks crowd the river, wings flapping noisily as they take-off. I've heard the familiar hollow patter of a woodpecker, and witnessed as many as four herons in one sitting. There are mammals, too. A water vole making a hasty retreat into the banks, squeaking loudly in indignation; a grey squirrel scampering up the trunk of the tree. The woodland even hides a herd of roe deer. I learned this the hard way, when the two dogs I was taking for a walk went flying after them, barking furiously – the worst part being that the dogs in question belonged to the professor who was just about to mark my master's thesis.

Having moved to the suburbs to the west of the city, I walk to my PhD office from further up the river's course. It's a beautiful part of the Don, surrounded by a thick border of trees and steep, grassy banks covered in wild flowers. A wooden boardwalk takes you right along the water's edge, giving off a pleasant clunk as your feet strike it. It is the perfect place to observe nature through the seasons. In autumn, the rich, russet tones of the trees are reflected in the water; in spring and summer, the place is vibrant and alive with birds and insects, a stark contrast to the muted tones and stillness of winter. It was here, wandering along the banks of the Don, that I saw my first otter, and I was lucky enough to follow her journey as the seasons changed.

I had heard whispers of an otter, sighted at various points along

Eurasian otter.

the Don, and I was dying to see one. The Eurasian otter (otherwise known as the 'common' or 'river' otter) symbolises Scottish wildlife. Although – as their name suggests – they are found across Europe, Scotland is a stronghold for this species with Shetland hosting one of the densest populations on the continent. We've come to associate their furry, be-whiskered faces with western Scotland, where they dwell in coastal areas – somewhat uniquely in comparison to the rest of the world's population. This has led to the nickname of 'sea otter' even though they are the exact same species as those inhabiting freshwater habitats further inland.

Otters are undeniably characteristic. They have a sweet face with round, chocolate button eyes and a snub nose, fringed with long white whiskers. Their expression is an inquisitive one, and they are playful by nature making them extremely fun to watch. Cubs play on the banks, slipping and sliding and tumbling over one another, whereas the adults splash and glide through the water. They seem to have endless energy, forever scrambling about the grass at the water's edge or swimming against the current in search of a tasty trout for supper. But, perhaps most enticing of all, is that seeing one in the wild is a rare occurrence. Eurasian otters are solitary and usually nocturnal, hunting by night and snuggling down in their 'holt' – the proper name for an otter's den – by day. But things it seems are topsy-turvy at the Don, as I caught sight of one in broad daylight.

My first sighting occurred in early summer. For once we had enjoyed a spell of deliciously warm, sunny weather, and the parks and hedgerows had responded wholeheartedly. Seaton park was triumphant with flowers in carnival colours, and the flower beds hummed with bees and insects. Cherry blossom drifted down the path in droves like the aftermath of a wedding, and the sunlight danced off the surface of the water. It was one of those days where the world seems to be brighter, more vibrant; there is something in the air that whispers of good times ahead. During those hazy summer days, I can't bring myself to sit in my stuffy little office and always find myself escaping to the river, where I can happily while away the hours that I should be working.

That day, I followed the path to one of my favourite spots – where the track heads up into the woods, a smaller dirt track branches off and slopes downwards. Take it, and you will find yourself at a tiny, secluded bay, sheltered by crooked hazel trees that stoop over an overhang; their twisted, gnarled roots exposed by hollows in the dirt. Here, the river is widening out and becoming calmer, settling down from the rapids further upstream. It is the perfect place to sit and reflect, to waste away the time in the most pleasant of ways.

I was perched on a rock beside the water's edge, watching the river lap lazily at the pebbles and the dappled patterns made as the sunlight shone through the leaves of the trees overhead. A male mallard duck was my only company, bobbing about like a cork in the middle of the water. With their teal-coloured heads and little white collar, I always think they look like a member of the clergy; pompous and slightly uncomfortable as if the collar is fitted just that little bit too tight. The warm air and gentle babble of the river was lulling me into a sleepy stupor, and my eyes were glazing over ... but then something shot out of the bank beside me and jolted me right out of it. The thing was about the size of a small cat and darkish in colour. Out of the corner of my eye, I could see it standing frozen and watching me intently, clearly realising it was not alone but unsure as to how to handle the situation. Ever so cautiously I turned my head, and saw an otter staring right back at me.

For a wee while the pair of us just looked at each other, both apparently in a bit of shock at the other's presence. I was too scared

A male mallard duck cruising down the river.

to move in case I frightened her, so instead I sat still as a statue and took it all in. Her body, sleek and streamlined, was the colour of milk chocolate all over except for her cream throat and chest. Her eyes were almost feline, glossy black and shining. Her button nose twitched as she tried to decide whether I was friend or foe, all four clawed feet splayed wide and ready to make a quick getaway. I don't know how long we remained like this – probably just a few magical minutes. Clearly bored by our encounter, she turned away and slid easily into the water.

Gently, I rose to my feet and watched as she dipped into the river, surfing the current. She was now much darker in colour; her pelt almost black and glistening with droplets. Their fur is water repellent, and consists of two layers, an inner layer, which is dense and snuggly warm, and a waterproof outer layer. Water simply runs off, and gives the otter a distinctly spikey appearance when they return to shore. Much like a decent waterproof jacket, this requires a fair bit of maintenance and otters are meticulous in keeping it well-groomed and healthy. In doing so, they manage to keep air trapped in between the layers, which helps them to keep warm whilst swimming and when drying out. Anyone who has tried their hand at water sports will understand the importance of this – standing by the side of the road in a wetsuit after a morning's surfing is probably one of my least favourite experiences of all time.

The otter began to swim upstream, and I followed. Every so often she would duck beneath the current and I would lose sight of her, but she would always reappear a few feet away. She was probably on the lookout for food, heading into the faster moving water in the hopes of catching a juicy trout or salmon. I did wonder, afterwards, if she was out to get food to feed cubs back at the den, the entrance to which must have been right beside where I was sitting. The Eurasian otter does not have a distinct breeding season – they breed throughout the year, and it is thought that instead breeding depends on the individual's sexual maturity at that time – so this could well have been the case. It was at the small band of rapids that I lost sight of her completely; the glare of the sun off the water was too great to see much, and although I stood for a wee while longer, I did not see her again. I had, however, spent a good half an hour watching this otter – time very well spent, and relatively long for a sighting like that – so I still went home a very happy conservationist. I had read somewhere that female otters established a core area where they set up home and tended to stay, so I could only hope that the Don was 'home' for this female.

The next time I saw her was quite some time later, towards the end of October. There was a brisk chill that stung my cheeks as my feet thunked along the boardwalk, and the air smelt of bonfires and wood smoke. The trees had exchanged their luscious green uniform for one of amber and burgundy, the colours reflecting in the glassy waters of the river. It was that time of year where winter threatened; the colour seemed to be leaching out of everything, and a thick carpet of soggy leaves covered the path. Birds and other wildlife were busying themselves, preparing for the harsh months ahead – the birds neglecting song in favour of hunting for morsels that would fatten them up. A granite flash streaked across the path in front of me; our most well-known invader, the grey squirrel. He zipped up the nearest tree, bushy tail held aloft for balance, and vanished amongst the branches ahead.

Suddenly, I heard a short, piercing cry, like a sharp blow on a whistle. Short and persistent, the sound was ten times louder than any bird call, its echoes reverberating across the river. For a while I stood still and scanned the area, listening to these shrill blasts, trying to identify their origin. And then I saw her – the otter! She was scrambling about on the opposite bank, seemingly frantic about something and uttering that harsh, bleating cry. I wondered what she was so worried about. Apparently trying a different tactic, she stopped clambering about the reeds and dived into the water, where she began to speed downstream, calling at intervals. I suddenly realised how streamlined an otter was; she moved at such speed I almost had to break into a jog to keep up.

As we reached the point where the river turned a corner and broke into rapids, I discovered the reason for her panic. For, waiting patiently on the banks by the riverbend, were two cubs! I could hardly believe my luck. They looked of a fair age; slightly smaller than the female and much fluffier, with a reddish tinge to their coat. Judging from their mother's reaction, the pair had been a little bit naughty and strayed too far from her side. She clambered up the bank and hastily checked them over, touching noses and fussing - I like to think she reprimanded them for their unruly behaviour. Then, having been royally told off, the cubs began to play, gambolling and tumbling over one another in the reeds. It was lovely to watch, and I stood there until my toes numbed and fingers stung with the cold.

It wasn't long until I saw the family again. December had arrived and with it, winter. The trees were now stripped of their foliage; barren skeletons, with their branches like crooked fingers reaching up into the sky. The colour palette was one of cool hues in greys and blues – with the odd pop of deep emerald from the evergreens – and wildlife sightings were thin on the ground. That day the temperature had dropped significantly and a thick layer of frost had settled, painting beautiful, intricate patterns on the wooden handrail of the boardwalk and causing the grass to crunch underfoot. Despite the cold, a pale, lemon coloured sun hung high in the sky, making the frost sparkle and casting everything with a magical quality.

The Don in winter.

I spotted the female otter almost immediately. Drifting on her back with the current, she was clutching a prized possession between her two front paws – a fish! I couldn't see well enough to decipher the species, but I guessed it would be a trout; the Don is a hotspot for recreational salmon and trout fishing, and there is nearly always an angler or two somewhere along the river. The mother otter alternated between swimming on her back and her front, transferring the fish from paw to jaw seamlessly, the scales glinting silver as she did so. With her was one cub, swimming circles around her – but where was the other? Could he or she be back at the holt? Or had they headed out on an adventure of their own?

As I walked I came across a cyclist leaning against the handrail, bike balanced carefully against his legs. He too, was watching the otters, and as he saw me approach he commented how sad it was about the other cub. Alarmed, I asked what had happened to it.

'Hit by a car just up by the bridge,' he replied. 'Some kind soul took it to the vet, but I have no idea whether it made it.'

Obviously, this was incredibly sad news. We stood and reflected on this for a while, the sorrow shared between us as we watched the mother and her remaining cub carry on downstream. Unfortunately, fatalities on the road are one of the biggest threats facing Scotland's otter population. We could only hope that the second cub would survive the hit. There was however, some good news. As we spoke, a buzzard – Scotland's most common bird of prey – swept across the water and settled in a tree on the adjacent side. It's always a pleasure to see these magnificent birds, with their beautiful mottled brown plumage and graceful flight. At this moment, the biker told me he had been cycling the Don route to work for fifty years, and had seen its progress from industrial waste site to wildlife haven. The river itself, he said, had got clearer and cleaner and the wildlife had followed; a few tentative garden birds at first, building up to the variety that we see today – a true conservation success story.

I smiled to myself, and reflected again on my fortune as having this as my walk to work. The Don will always be a special place to me, but has been made even more so for the little family of otters that called it home.

Tips and tricks for otter spotting...

* Spotting an otter can be a tricky business – like all British mammals, they tend to be wary and are easily frightened away. The perfect recipe includes the ideal habitat (a combination of river or coastline, marshy wetland, lakes and reedbeds, with plentiful insects and fish), a good sprinkling of patience, and a dash of luck.

* River otters are predominantly nocturnal, so the best time to catch sight of one is at dawn or dusk. Find a comfy spot with a flask of tea and sit quietly – the otter will patter out in its own time.

* During the day, you can look out for tell-tale signs in the soft mud of the river banks such as webbed pawprints. Spraints – otter poop, to you and me – will contain fish bones and be placed at strategic locations around the holt. Apparently, the scent is something like jasmine tea, although I am yet to be convinced of that...

* Coastal otters are generally more active during the day, as the prey is plentiful at these sites. Pick the right spot, and you will often see them clambering about the seaweed, munching on fish or even a crab or two.

* As always with wildlife, be respectful – maintain your distance, and bear in mind otters are easily disturbed, especially next to the holt.

Otter hangouts

* **Cricklepit Mill (Exeter):** As well as having a name that rolls nicely off the tongue, this urban area is easily accessible and boasts regular sightings

* **Aughton woods (Lancashire):** The river Lune is an otter hotspot, and has the added bonus of being surrounded by beautiful ancient woodland

* **Westhay Moor (Somerset):** Idyllic otter habitat, which has proved an important site for the species

* **Staveley (Yorkshire):** Famous for its mother-and-cub sightings

* **Kylerhea otter hyde (Isle of Skye):** enjoy amazing views over the narrows whilst observing the shoreline

* **Isle of Mull:** the Mull otter group do not release otter locations (to stop them receiving too much attention), but it is one of the best places to see coastal otters in the country. Have a wander and see what you can find!

Swallow feeding her chicks.

Swallows and Martins

I n Britain we are lucky enough to have the changing seasons – four of them, to be exact – something which I think is one of our best features. Some might disagree with me; it seems we spend half of our time miserable in an apparently endless winter, and the other half being practically giddy at the merest whisper of summer. But every season brings with it little triumphs to celebrate, with its own unique set of sensory delights to savour and enjoy. Winter may be bleak, but it can be beautiful – the sounds of the wind rattling the scraggly trees and the crunch of frost underfoot; the smoky, woody scent of bonfires cutting through the crisp, pure air that makes the eyes water and your breath rise into misty tendrils. Spring is the sudden explosion of colour and life following the darkness of winter, and as the air warms becomes thick with the heady aroma of wild garlic, honeysuckle and freshly cut grass, the melodies of birds and the busy hum of insects. summer speaks of long days spent at the beach getting accidentally sunburnt, and lazy evening walks as the sun refuses to go to bed like an indignant child. The air smells of sea salt and warm foliage, the colours a palette of cornflower blue and various shades of luscious green, interspersed with purples and pinks and buttercup yellow. Finally, as we move into autumn, this colour scheme turns into bonfire hues – burgundy, burnt orange and gold – mixed with the scent of damp leaves and rich, cloying earth.

Furthermore, as the seasons turn, so does the composition and behaviour of the wildlife and for each one, there are a few species which have become an integral part of the identity of that season. Autumn, for example, is frantic as everyone prepares for the darkness ahead; small mammals, like squirrels and weasels, scurry about by day, and during the night hedgehogs bumble and urban foxes stalk the shadows. Enormous, hairy wolf spiders stalk their way indoors and the last of the wasps stumble drunkenly through windows. Easily the icon of winter is the robin with his resplendent red breast, but also for me the red deer. The great stags rut well into November, their roaring calls unfurling into mist. Spring, of course, has chicks and lambs. But summer has so much to choose from it's hard to whittle it down to a few species. The period of May to September is the ideal time to spot so many, from whales and dolphins to a variety of delicate butterflies and moths of all different shapes, sizes and

Swallow and house martin comparison.

patterns. But my favourite summer icons come from a little family of birds called the Hirundinidae; the swallows and martins.

This little group are arguably some of our prettiest birds. They are small and elegant, their wings tapered and delicately pointed, accompanied by a distinctive forked tail. These birds are famous for their serious skills in the air and are astonishingly agile, performing aerial acrobatics at high speed. You will often see them swooping and swerving, changing direction with the rapidity and capability of stunt riders. They are built for a diet of winged insects; the epitome of 'fast food'. They will snatch their prey right out of the sky and gulp it down, sometimes even mid-flight. As such their beaks are small but wide, perfect for catching food on the go, but this also lends them a distinctly sweet appearance especially when coupled with their wide, round, beetle-black eyes. As a family, they are 'migrant breeders': arriving to breed in late March, before heading off to their wintering grounds in Africa. They always herald the beginning of summer for me. We have three main species to enjoy in the UK, and I have had the privilege of having encounters with all of them. They may look similar, but each one has distinguishing features and habitat preferences that set them apart.

Let's start with the celebrity of the group – swallows. They are certainly the most widely known, being the focus of popular tattoo designs and fashion prints, but they have also become synonymous with Summer. They are normally found on or near bodies of water. I see them most often in the lake behind my brother's house, where they zoom across skimming its surface for insects. Swallows are particularly fond of quiet, largely undisturbed pasture on or adjacent to wetland, and one summer I caught sight of a group dancing about a derelict farmhouse in the fields not so far from my 'home home' in Whitley Bay. It was dusk; the sky striped with rose pink and orange and the air thick with the sweet scents of summer – that heady, floral mixture of cow parsley, jasmine and wild herbs. The swallows were out in force, zipping about me so fast it almost made me dizzy. In the dim light I could just make out their colouring – the deep blue-black upper-parts, contrasting starkly with the crisp white underside. If I squinted, I could even make out their characteristic scarlet throat. But the most distinctive feature of all stood out like a sore thumb, silhouetted against the sky; a narrow, deeply forked tail with long 'streamers' on either side, like an oddly shaped kite. They are the most beautiful things to watch; pirouetting and divebombing, flipping round corners and calling to one another in a series of cheerful chirps and rapid bursts of clicks. I stood and watched as long as the midges would allow – an unfortunate consequence of the age-old recipe of humidity and wetlands.

Back when my niece was little, we used to head out to collect tadpoles from an expansive pond a short walk from my brother's abode, which is situated right beside the Tyne valley. She would waddle along the path, one hand slipped inside mine and the other tightly clutching a plastic jug, in which she would transport the tadpoles back to the house with the exaggerated care of a butler carrying the Queen's jewels. We would always see the swallows, which she would watch with her sky blue eyes held wide as they zig-zagged across the pond water. On one rare occasion, we even managed to sneak up on one having a brief rest on a reed stem, and watched as its tiny white chest hitched up and down, its back shimmering iridescent blue in the sunlight.

House martins and swifts sometimes get confused for swallows.

The colourful swallow with its forked tail.

Being associated more with urban environments than freshwater, I'll come back to house martins later in the book. But in short, they tend to be stockier in shape, with a shorter tail that has a less obvious fork. They share the colouration – darker upper plumage with white underparts – but lack the crimson face. Another common mistake is thinking a swallow is a swift, and vice versa. Superficially, swifts are extremely similar with forked tails, bullet-shaped bodies and scythe-shaped wings. But they are in fact from a completely different family, the Apodidae, and have a few characteristics on which to tell them apart. Their bodies are almost completely a dark, muddy shade of brown, making them appear black against the sky. Like martins and swallows, they are extremely agile flyers but tend to go much higher. Look up above the rooftops at dusk and you may see great parties of them, screaming to one another excitedly in high-pitched, sharp bursts. Swifts have a reputation for being the 'red-bull' of the bird world, fizzing with so much energy they barely stop – they've even been known to catch a bit of shut-eye mid-flight. It may come as no surprise that they are related to hummingbirds whose wings beat so fast they become a blur of feather.

If swallows are the country bumpkins of the family, then house martins are the city mice. Traditionally, they used to nest on cliff faces, like fulmars or puffins – but by the 1990s, they began to take advantage of the urban sprawl occurring further inland and chose a less 'daredevil' way of life. They make use of the nooks and crannies of buildings, commonly nesting underneath the eaves on the outer walls, and are often seen vanishing into the façade in the evenings. Most people enjoy their summer house guests, but some are confused by the appearance of these weird new ornaments adorning the walls of their house.

Throughout my late teens, especially once I'd gone to uni, I got a bit of a reputation for myself as an animal nerd amongst my friends and family back at home. Frequently I was called upon to identify this beetle or that butterfly, or queried as to how best nurse a startled bird back to health after it had collided with a window. I'd been asked my advice on how to stop a dog from barking at strangers, who to phone about a lost seal pup, and countless times to remove an unwanted insect from indoors. Unwittingly, I'd become my neighbourhood's resident wildlife enthusiast.

One summer holiday, back in Newcastle after a long uni term, I got a call from one of my close friends asking me to come over and 'check out the weird blobs on the house'. Weird blobs?! On a house?? Intrigued, I jumped straight on my bike and headed to the scene of the crime. Her family were in some sort of panic, convinced a killer breed of wasps or something equally unfriendly had descended on their home. They took me to the part of the house where the garage connected to the gables, querulously speculating as to what aliens had landed. There, in a secluded spot where the roof overhung the side of the house, were three little bowl-shaped clumps of earth, perfectly rounded and shaped to the angle of the wall. On each one, close to the top, was a small hole, exactly spherical. Immediately I knew this was no wasp nest; it wasn't the right size or shape, and that hole was too big. Plus – as I explained to the worried faces of my friend's family – there was no menacing buzz, but a very faint chirping noise. Their aliens were, in fact, house martins.

House martins in flight.

To cement this fact, I climbed up some stepladders and took a closer peek. The nests were mostly mud, but peering inside the hole I could see they were lined with grass and feathers. And then – almost on cue – three tiny little feathered heads protruded through the hole and began to wheeze madly at me, their blackberry eyes wide and imploring, canary yellow mouths held wide in anticipation. 'Oh, how sweet!' My friend's mam exclaimed, now extremely relieved the family was no longer in danger of severe wasp attack. I explained house martins are colonial breeders – they like to set up home in groups, almost like a little neighbourhood – it isn't uncommon to see up to five nests together. Gently, so as not to startle them further, I retreated back down the stepladder and we clustered underneath the nests, peering up at them as the three heads of the chicks vanished again back inside their muddy home. Five minutes later, however, they were back, wheezing even more frantically than before; the mother had returned, swooping low over our heads to settle on the side of the nest, her mouth full of some sort of leggy insect. Much like a swallow, she had darker upper plumage and snow white underparts, but she also had a white 'rump spot' at the base of her tail. House martins are also generally stockier in shape, with a shorter forked tail and the absence of the swallow's party streamers. If you can get close enough, you will also see their legs and toes are covered in feathers, as though they are wearing tiny furry trousers.

Having recovered from their initial fear of alien invasion, my friend's family welcomed their new lodgers with open arms – although none more so than her dad. The next time I went around I found him angling the garden hose to a spot on the driveway not far from the nests, humming joyfully to himself. Upon careful inquisition (I wasn't sure whether there was reason to the madness, or if he'd just been under a lot of pressure at work), I discovered he'd read that house martins, being entirely dependent on insects, will prefer a place where they aggregate. Since my last visit he'd been meticulously maintaining a puddle in the driveway, as dedicated as another dad would be to his garden plants.

Now we come to the third member of this little family. I have seen these a few times – once on a trip to the west coast, once on a wander to Montrose, and twice whilst walking down the pebbled banks of the river at Speyside.

My sightings at the latter two locations both began with one shared detail: a wide, sandy bank, crumbling in places and overhung with grass and clods of earth. At Speyside, the bank was carved from the land by the meandering course of the river; at Montrose, the man-made result of excavating the pond on which the kingfisher had perched proudly. At first glance, two completely normal sandbanks. Except when you look closer, something odd becomes apparent: the banks are covered in holes. Rows and rows of little uniform holes, perfectly rounded, making the banks look like a crumbly wedge of swiss cheese.

These are the burrows of sand martins. Their Latin name – *Riparia riparia* – literally translates as 'of banks', and they are true to the name. What appear as small holes can actually be one metre long tunnels, dug by the males and perfected into cosy nest chambers by the females. Once satisfied, they will lay up to five eggs and nestle them at the end of the burrow, where they will be protected from the elements and unwanted visitors. I watched them at the river Spey busily flitting in and out of their homes, squiggling insects clutched within their beaks. They are the smallest of all swallows, only about 12cm in length, and in contrast to their monochrome cousins are cappuccino brown with a cream underside. Look closely enough, and you might be able to see the distinctive hazelnut brown band across the breast. The forked tail is still there, but shorter, and their triangular wings are perfectly arched and tapered to the tip. They are slight, elegant birds, and would hover at the entrance to the burrow with their wings swept back and the spoils of their hunt thrust proudly into the hole.

Sand martins are very sociable birds and nest in colonies, like little neighbourhoods. They start to arrive on British soil in late March; breed and raise their young throughout the summer, before gathering to roost in autumn, when they group together to travel in great numbers to their wintering grounds in Africa. Sadly, it is this choice that has been their downfall. Droughts in Africa have caused the UK population to crash over the last fifty years and placed them in a worrying position. The artificial sand bank at Montrose – along with others being built across the UK – are conservation measures to provide safe refuge when they arrive, exhausted from their mammoth journey. Similarly managing our existing wetlands 'sympathetically', leaving their most important habitats intact, is equally as important. At the river Spey, it was great to see well over a hundred little holes, from which the martins would busily flit backwards and forwards, disappearing inside at intervals.

On the west coast of Scotland, pristine wetland habitats are in rich supply. Whilst on holiday just outside of Fort William in the joyfully named Kilmalieu, we squelched our way through bogs and marshland to a small loch nestled amongst heather-covered hills and clumps of ancient woodland. Here, we found a group of sand martins, no doubt feasting on the midges who thrive in the warm, moist air surrounding bodies of water in summer. They may be smaller than house martins or common swallows, but they still have all the speed and agility. The sand martins sped around the corners of the loch, sometimes coming so close to the surface that it was a wonder they didn't crash into it. Skimming low over the water, they would zoom to the edge before – like the most skilled of jet fighters – pulling a hard corner, flipping back on themselves in mid-air and careering in the other direction. They were capturing insects on the wing, pirouetting and calling to each other in celebration with little repetitive, bubbly bursts of sound.

Perhaps it is the sheer energy and joy of all four of these species that makes them so synonymous with the summer months. They truly encapsulate the spirit of this season – spiralling and dancing and careering about in celebration, and often carrying on well into dusk. And the best thing about them is, they are not hard to find. Swallows are never far away – just find your nearest body of water, nearby to pasture. Sand martins may take a bit more effort but are well worth it, peeking out of their nest chambers with those big Bambi eyes and small, delicately-featured faces. Even if our summer only lasts four days – which sometimes is the harsh reality – these little birds will be enough to lift your spirits up with them, bringing the essence of the season with every graceful swoop and swerve.

Sand martin skimming the loch at Kilmalieu.

Mute swans gliding across the surface of the new wetland in Seaton Park, Aberdeenshire.

Wetland: a refuge in the city

There is a very old saying which I'm sure you are familiar with; *there is a silver lining to every cloud*. Put simply it means that even in the darkest of days, when the most thunderous of clouds roll overhead, there is always a glimmer of hope. When things get bad there is always something to cling to. I like to think this applies to wildlife as well. They are, for the most part, having to make the most of one bad situation or another; evolving and adapting to the changes thrust upon them and their environment. I am always astonished at how, even when things are at their bleakest, our wildlife can create its own silver lining.

There was a time in Aberdeenshire when that saying was (quite literally) put to the test. Just after Christmas we experienced some of the worst rain and storms on record. The rain came in droves and seemed interminable; a never-ending and relentless downpour that soaked into the earth until it reached saturation point and caused floods across the county. It started suddenly and without warning, bringing destruction with it. Roads were washed away, whole houses crumbled, trees felled in the accompanying gale-force winds and puddles morphed into flowing rivers that cascaded down the streets, carrying cars with them. For a brief time, Aberdeen was completely cut off from the rest of Scotland with major roads and railways shut down – even flights were affected.

It was a worrying time for a lot of people. Thankfully, I lived far enough away from any rivers that all I had to deal with was a slight leak in the ceiling and some soggy shoes. But people in other places weren't so lucky. Many lost their houses and businesses to the floods, and for months the damage and devastation was apparent. Another troubling aspect was the wildlife – how would our flora and fauna cope? With whole chunks of river bank swept away and ground waterlogged, would their homes survive? One of the worst affected places was the Donmouth nature reserve. Not soon after the storm began, the river – already swollen following the snowmelt and normal rains of winter – burst its banks, sweeping across the flat land of the park like spilt paint across canvas. In the aftermath, the park was a scene of chaos; branches and leaves strewn across it and whole trees splintered in half, their carcasses blocking the path in places. The grass was incredibly boggy and squelchy underfoot, and in parts the fields and flower beds were completely submerged under great lakes of water. A lone robin perched atop a scraggly branch sticking out of one of the new-found reservoirs, looking rather like a survivor of a sunken boat who had become trapped on a raft, his crimson chest a tiny life jacket.

But what began as a sorry state of affairs slowly became something beautiful. As time went on, the water levels receded and the Don retreated to its usual size. The wayward branches were cleared, and the enormous trunks of fallen oak and horse chestnut trees attracted insects and squirrels, crawling and scampering about the holes and crevices. One of the things I used to adore as a kid was a felled tree. I loved to look at its now-exposed root system; the little rootlets stretching out and twisting over each other, covered in clumps of dirt and earth. Only then can you appreciate the mammoth size of these structures, which are normally hidden beneath the ground. I liked to insect hunt inside the hollow trunk, finding millipedes with their rippling fringe of legs; great, shiny black beetles with waggling antennae and wolf spiders, stalking their prey along the base of the trunk with all the ferocity of a lion in the savannah.

However, the biggest and possibly brightest silver lining was somewhere else. To the right of the Don is an enormous field, normally used for nothing more than football matches on Saturday afternoons and as a spot of respite for tired parents during the holidays. Despite its proximity to the reserve, I never saw much in the way of wildlife there, apart from a few seagulls, hopeful for whatever scraps they could glean from an errant toddler. But following the storm, something wonderful happened – the field turned itself into a wetland habitat. Everywhere else, the floods had dried up, leaving no trace except a squelchy sound if you stood on it too hard. But here the field stood in a sort of basin, bordered on all sides by steep slopes of land and trees, and the flood had stayed. The ground was beyond saturation point and so the water lay on top, creating a permanent lake and surrounding marshland. Clusters of reeds and furry little clumps of river grass had already begun to grow. And whole new host of wildlife had settled. The usual suspects were there – flocks of herring gulls, chattering noisily to each other and taking off in a great rustle of wings when startled; mallard ducks, the females in their demure pale brown and the males with their showier iridescent green heads. And magpies hopped mischievously about the banks, beady eyes on the lookout for any wayward bread crumbs. Amongst them, however, were the newcomers. A pair of mute swans glided across the water with the effortlessness and grace of two figure skaters; snow white except for their tangerine coloured bills. Mute swans always tend to look a little fierce thanks to the jet-black mask across their eyes, which flicks up at the corner like eyeliner from the 60s and gives the impression that they are constantly hacked off. You can use this to distinguish them from the whooper swans, which don't have the mask and generally look more amicable. Their bill is canary yellow and their legs jet black, as if they're wearing stockings.

There was also a lonesome tufted duck, drifting some distance away from the others. Their name comes from the long tuft of black feather that curves over the back of the head of the males, not unlike the ponytails sported by middle aged rock stars. In keeping with that theme, they are pitch black all over except for a white belly and silvery grey bill. The females – like many other bird species – are a tad more drab in colour, their plumage a warm reddish-brown. But the one startling feature they both share are a pair of luminous banana yellow eyes, perfectly round, like buttons. These give the tufted duck a look of constant surprise, as if life in general just startles them. This particular male kept himself to himself, those wide yellow eyes casting a terrified look at the gaggle of gulls, terns and swans that had accumulated in the middle of the water. Some children had gathered to feed the birds, throwing breadcrumbs into the lake. The swans arrived first, their s-shaped necks poised to grab the gifts hurled at them, followed closely by the mallards, a little less graceful, who pecked at the now soggy morsels as they drifted towards them. The ever-wary tufted duck eyed them in astonishment before turning and swimming in the opposite direction, seemingly shocked at the audacity of those more common wetland birds.

This new habitat – albeit an unexpected one – brought all kinds of different visitors. Throughout the winter months, I often wandered down to see what new arrivals I could spot. Some wading birds began to enjoy the new marshland; dippers, sand plovers and oystercatchers scurried through the reeds, picking at whatever beasties they could find. Once, I came across a red-breasted merganser, a spectacular looking duck. They are a member of the 'sawbill' family, so called because of their thin serrated beak – the perfect tool with which to dissect fish. They are of a similar colour scheme to a mallard duck with that familiar white collar and green-black head, shimmering iridescent when it catches the light. But the most interesting feature about this bird is the crazy spiked hairstyle it sports, a crest of frizzy thin feathers that jut out the back of the head like a mad professor. Red breasted mergansers are widely distributed about the UK at certain times of the year; usually residents of the west, and winter visitors of the east. Although comfortable in both salt water and fresh water habitats, they are usually found at the coast – so I was surprised to see such a guest to the wetland. Their usual diet consists of salmon and trout, and although the lake was certainly proving popular I'm not sure it housed fish as large as that. I could only assume he had stopped off for a little rest on his way to the sea front.

I would like to take a moment here to apologise for the fact that this chapter is a little duck-heavy – there is a reason the saying goes 'taking to it like a duck to water'. But this is the last one, I promise … and a pretty special one at that.

I never thought I'd be the type of person who got excited over the arrival of a rare duck, but, here we are. However, if you consider the fact that there have only been ten reported sightings of this species in the UK since 1950, it's a pretty exciting thing to a zoologist. I didn't actually know what I'd seen at the time. I remember thinking 'hmmm, what an odd-looking duck' and ashamedly didn't google it until about a week later, after more pressing issues – such as the latest assignment and an outstanding gas bill – had left my mind. Only then did I realise how excited I should have been.

Now, this was a bird that stood out – a duck that demanded attention. He stood knee deep in the water (I mean, that is, if ducks have knees … of this I am not quite sure) looking extremely out of place, like a peacock amongst chickens. His markings were striking; almost geometric in nature, starkly white on a background of blue-black with a chestnut patch each the side. A dot and a dash were situated just behind the eye, and two parallel markings ran down the middle of the head like a roman helmet. There were a further two white stripes around the throat and a series of triangular shapes towards the end of the wing. His head was shaped in a high arch, a

A male harlequin duck, a rare winter visitor to the UK.

maroon and white crest just protruding from the forehead. He was nothing if not distinctive, and certainly not anything I'd seen before. It wasn't long, however, before he took off and sped in the direction of the river to the west.

Later, I learnt this unfamiliar guest was in fact a harlequin duck. Native to Iceland and North America, it is an extremely scarce winter visitor to the UK, with only a handful of sightings to its name. The harlequin truly lives up to its name, being so vividly and colourfully dressed that I was able to remember its appearance a week later. I had heard whispers of a rare duck amongst the 'twitchers' at uni, but not thought anything of it. How on earth someone like me – an amateur birder at best – had stumbled upon it by happenstance was beyond me, and I counted myself as very lucky indeed.

It always amazes me how nature can colonise a new area so quickly, and make it their own. At that time, there was still evidence this used to be a human playground: a half-submerged bench, for example, or a sign reminding locals that there was 'no golf practice' allowed, right slap bang in the middle of the water. But the area has now been officially identified as a wetland habitat by the authorities, and the wildlife has taken to it … like ducks to water! This served as a strong reminder that what we may consider to be a 'bad' situation for us may be an ideal scenario for wildlife; finding their own silver lining in a sky full of clouds.

WWT Wetlands Centre, London.

The importance of wetlands

Wetlands are a vital part of the country's wider ecosystem health, not only supporting a vast array of wildlife but also lessening the more severe impacts of extreme weather events. But they are amongst our most threatened habitats. Often occurring in low-lying areas, they are susceptible to urban development and so frequently lost to new housing estates and infrastructure. However – as I experienced with Seaton park – they are easily restored and created, and provide some of the most important refuges for wildlife in urban areas. Here are some of the best:

* **WWT Wetlands Centre, London:** just ten minutes from Hammersmith, this is the world's first man-made wetland reserve and boasts an impressive assortment of species, including nesting sand martins, bitterns and a huge variety of bats.

* **Cley Marshes, Norfolk:** Labelled as a 'mecca for birdwatchers', this extensive habitat of reed beds and lagoons is the perfect place to spot any number of avian visitors.

* **Drumburgh Moss Nature Reserve, Cumbria:** An internationally significant site for 'raised mire' – one of Western Europe's most threatened habitats. See curlew, red grouse, adders and roe deer.

* **North Cave Wetlands, Yorkshire:** this reserve began life as a quarry, but is now a thriving mosaic of wetland habitat. Gulls, terns and great crested grebe enjoy its bounty, alongside a great variety of butterflies, dragonflies and damselflies.

* **Duddingston Loch, Edinburgh:** the only freshwater loch in the city. Sightings include waterfowl, breeding herons and even otters.

* **Knockshinnoch Lagoons Wildlife Reserve, Ayrshire:** the combination of lagoons, marshland and reed beds attracts a diverse array of summer breeding birds, such as rail, whinchat and reed bunting.

Osprey.

Dragons great and small

Every summer since second year, a group of university friends and I embark on an adventure. At first, we made tentative excursions to nearby places in my friend's rickety little Clio, which struggled to get uphill with five passengers and would judder worryingly along the dual carriageway, needing some serious coaxing to reach sixty miles an hour. Once we grew older and our transportation improved (well, there was less danger of breaking down in the middle of nowhere) our horizons broadened and we travelled further afield: Skye, Fort William, the Cairngorms. Post-graduation, organising our adventures has become nothing short of a military operation. We have scattered across the UK like dandelion seeds, so the location must be somewhere vaguely 'in the middle'. Additionally, the sad nature of adulthood means the majority are in full-time work – we can no longer leave at the drop of a hat where previously adventures had followed an idea half-formed in the pub. Instead, we have to wait for that tiny window of opportunity when we are all free. But still, we make this valiant effort every year and it is always worth the blood, sweat and tears that goes into its administration.

One year, our travels took us to an ideal 'meet in the middle' – the Lake District. The five of us piled into a squeaky new hire car and bumbled our way through the countryside, snaking around the multiple twists and bends that took us through rolling hills and meadows. We passed placid reservoirs and racing streams, ramshackle dry-stone walls and farmer's fields bordered by thick hedgerows, filled with blank-faced sheep. Sheep are a regular fixture of the Lakes, a spray of white dots across the grass-green of the landscape. Twice we had the rather unusual experience of being stuck in a traffic jam – not behind a tractor or broken down van, as you might expect, but instead a huge flock of sheep, a jostling amalgamation of cotton wool and confused bleating. The shepherd, ruddy faced and seemingly very relaxed, simply raised his flat cap by way of apology and then began a conversation with the car behind about the weather and the new sausages at the butchers. Having lived in Aberdeen – where road rage was almost part of the language – this was a novel experience for us to say the least, and one which we still find hilarious.

During that week, we were treated to a true British summer. Rain drove down in sheets and lashed against our windows; the wind screeched around the gables of our little rental cottage. We did try to make the most, one day braving Helvellyn – with its infamous leg-trembling ridge – and almost got blown off the summit. That evening, as we thawed out in front of the fire and watched a thrush literally get washed off his perch, we made the reluctant decision to remain indoors with the tennis the following day, hunkered down with hot chocolate to weather out the storm (which, incidentally, it felt like we were sitting in the eye of). The day after that, however, we awoke to an eerie stillness. The sun filtered in through the blinds and cast the room with a golden glow, and the birds chirruped cheerfully without even a whisper of a breeze. It was as though the storm had never happened, and we had woken in a parallel universe where 'summer' actually existed. This, we decided, was a day for ospreys.

Say the word 'spectacular' and it immediately brings ospreys to mind. They are one of our most magnificent birds of prey, with a wingspan of almost 1.7m (5½ft) and famed for their dramatic fishing technique of plunging into the river or lake, talons first, in a great spray of water. Their appearance is also very striking. White, mottled underparts can be seen from below, whilst the wings and back are chocolate brown with a distinctive 'patch' at the angled joint of the wings. Their face is one of a perfect predator – yellow, almond shaped eyes with a piercing gaze, and a formidable hooked beak. The osprey's diet is exclusively fish, and this tool serves as an efficient device with which to fillet and tear, and looks suitably fearsome. To complete the look, the osprey has a characteristic 'highway man's' mask across the eyes, from which those eyes gleam luminously. To me, they are the epitome of what it means to be a 'bird of prey'; every single feature primed for hunting with speed and power. I'd seen one a long time ago, at the age of about six or seven, on a family holiday to Scotland and the experience had clung fiercely to memory. At the time, I was fascinated by dragons and the osprey – circling the loch with its wings arched – could almost be one. Add that to the fact that a thin veil of mist hung over the scene, and you have a very magical image that stayed with me to this day.

Our site of choice was a place called Bassenwhaite lake, where the birds had first arrived back in 2001. The history of the osprey in Britain is a tumultuous one. Once common in Scotland and, some think, England (there is reference to the species in works by Shakespeare and John Skelton), they were hunted to extinction in the eighteenth and nineteenth centuries, with the last recorded pair destroyed in 1916. However, intensive conservation measures saw the return of the osprey to Scotland in the 1950s, where it now has a stronghold. The arrival of ospreys to the Lake District was the culmination of several years of impressive work. A nest platform was built in Wythop woods, which allowed a pair to naturally colonise the

Wythop woods.

A babbling brook in the middle of the woods.

area after almost a century of absence. It was here my friends and I were headed on that gorgeous July day, with the cornflower blue sky reeling above us, to witness dragons.

The route to the nest platform involves a steep hike up through Wythop woods, a thick forest of towering Douglas firs rising high over the hill, and clumps of shield ferns, their fronds drooping over the path. There was a closeness to the forest; the air thick with the scent of pine needles and warm earth. The sunlight coming through the dense canopy of evergreens cast everything in an emerald light, and the woods were filled with bird song. Somewhere in the distance, a woodpecker's hollow knocking echoed through the trees; close by, the merry call of a chiff-chaff cut through the dense air. Up we climbed, our feet cushioned by a thick carpet of fallen needles and leaves, stopping every now and again to listen out for a bird call or to inspect the undergrowth for beasties.

After a hefty half an hour hike, the wall of firs opened into a clearing. The path was now bordered by dusky pink primrose and thick tangles of brambles, hung with intricate spider webs. Enormous bumblebees thrummed their way from flower to flower, whilst smaller, golden honeybees zig-zagged drunkenly through the prickly shrubs. They would disappear now and again into the deep mauve bell of a foxglove, their busy silhouettes just visible through the crepe-thin petals. It is always a good omen to see bees. If the environment was a machine, bees and other pollinators are the vital cogs that keep it turning – without them, the whole thing would collapse. Perhaps one of the scariest issues facing conservation today is the fact that many species of bee are in decline, suffering due to habitat loss and degradation. A world without bees is a very scary prospect indeed. The finely tuned balance of our ecosystem would tip, and the effects would ripple out like a stone thrown into a pond. Bees and other pollinators play an essential role in the fertilisation and growth of flowering plants, ferrying pollen from one plant to another as they go about their busy day. Removing them from the planet would

mean the downfall of so many plants, and it doesn't take a genius to figure out that's a very bad thing. We can help them by planting and encouraging the growth of wildflowers and other 'bee-friendly' plants – wild herbs (thyme, marjoram), fragrant bushes of lavender and bergamot, and other wild plants with lovely sounding names such as honeysuckle, hyssop and sweet William (try saying them out loud ... it's very satisfying). The path at Wythop woods was alive with bees of all different shapes and sizes, humming to themselves as they went about their work. This has to be one of the happiest sounds of the natural world, that speaks of lazy summer days spent dosing outdoors. Although, possibly, not for my best friend Jen, who lives in terror of anything that buzzes.

We arrived at the viewing platform hot and wiping the sweat from our foreheads, but hopeful. The view from the platform was breath-taking, looking down into the valley with the lake, glassy and expansive, nestled at the bottom. The sun was high in the sky causing the water to sparkle, and gilding the patchwork landscape of arable land, meadows and pockets of forest. The platform is manned by a series of hard-working volunteers; waiting for us was an endlessly tall man, with a kindly, well-weathered face that crinkled at the eyes. Much to our delight he informed us that not only were ospreys present but there was also a chick in the nest, and directed us to three telescopes angled perfectly towards it. Peering down through the eyepiece, there it was – the nest, carefully placed in the crux of two crooked branches atop a scraggly, bare tree. It was enormous, a huge mass of moss, bark and twigs spilling over the boughs. The female usually perches on the side of the eyrie to feed her brood, and

Buff-tailed bumblebees visit the flowers.

Foxgloves.

Bassenwhaite lake. The view of the valley from the osprey viewing platform.

that's where we found her, standing tall and regal as she surveyed the land about her. I hadn't expected to see an osprey straight off the bat like this, and I almost caught my breath. Her great wings were folded behind her back, her head turning gracefully from side to side as she kept watch, those bright yellow eyes in stark contrast with the dark mask behind them. Sometimes, the cream coloured plumage on an osprey's forehead is distinctly 'fluffy', giving an almost spiked punk hairdo. It was particularly prominent on this female, a white fluffy halo that seemed to soften her fiercer features.

Duncan, our wise informant, had been monitoring these ospreys since the project began and was an expert on their ecology. The female went by the mysterious name of 'KL', and was the proud mother of seven-week-old Bega. At this age, Bega was beginning to find her wings and on the verge of fledging. As we watched, she poked her head up from the nest cup, the small feathers fringing her face sticking up like a lion's mane. She rose, shaking herself off,

and perched unsteadily on the edge of the nest. Then, with her face the epitome of determination, she began to vigorously flap her wings whilst facing into the wind for lift. All the while her talons gripped furiously onto the sticks to prevent actual take-off – seemingly, Bega was not quite ready to leave home just yet. This behaviour is known as 'helicoptering' and is used by juvenile birds to test out the strength of their wings and prepare for actual flight, much like riding a bike with stabilisers before going it alone on two wheels. A few months later, Bega would eventually leave the eyrie and head out on her own. Young ospreys usually travel for the first few years of their life; our native birds will normally winter in West Africa, and return to the UK between the ages of 2 and 7.

During this little flight practice, KL had taken off and flown in the direction of the lake. She sped back and forth across the landscape, becoming a white streak against the green-brown palette of the hills. Every now and again she would stop and hover high above the water,

A perfectly placed telescope.

searching for the sign of a fish to capture. Each time we would wait with baited breath, hoping to see a hunt in action, but suddenly she would speed off again and we would have to strain our eyes through the binoculars to follow her. Sometimes she would fly behind a clump of forest or the aggressively white-washed church which stood bright and proud in the distance, and we would lose sight of her altogether. This is when Duncan came in handy; he could always find her again within seconds, sometimes even without binoculars. I began to wonder whether all that extra height gave him an advantage...

We continued to avidly watch the female, and she swooped back and forth and made great, sweeping laps around the lake. My binocular skills were not up to the whip-smart accuracy of Duncan's and I would often find myself following the completely wrong bird, or end up in a different part of the valley to everyone else. Nevertheless, I had them locked firmly on the osprey when she began to descend towards the water, wings stretched wide as she rode the wind down towards her target. Then, at the very last moment, she swung them back so that they stood vertically, almost like a butterfly at rest with its wings folded carefully to its back. Except this was no delicate movement, but a ferocious one. With her talons spread wide and stretched out in front of her in anticipation, she collided with the water, sending up an arch of spray that glittered with rainbows in the high sun of the afternoon. I caught my breath. It was a dramatic climax; one of those moments in which time seemed to slow, stretching seconds into minutes and causing the hairs to stand up and prickle on your arms.

For a snapshot in time she was submerged, then, as the water settled, she began to flap those tremendous wings to heave herself and the fish out of the water, and take to the skies once more. Watching those powerful muscles flex, you could really appreciate how much effort it took to get airborne – not least when weighed down with something of half your body weight. With every great sweep, she lifted herself a little higher, sending out ripples across the surface of the lake. Then suddenly, she was clear of the water with the slippery form of a fish clutched tightly in her talons. Moving to the more powerful abilities of the telescope, you could even see the fish gasping desperately for air, its eyes wide and frantic as it realised its fate. The osprey had never seemed more dragon-like than in that moment, with her wings arched above her back, neck hung low and those glowing yellow eyes fixated on her next destination. She carted the fish back to the nest where she and Bega tore apart their spoils, blissfully undisturbed. It is a beautiful thing to see animals who were once made absent from our lands back in their natural environment, and being so successful. In a few months, Bega would be a fully-fledged adult in her own right, catching her own dinner and undertaking epic migrations to far-away countries. Hopefully one day she would return to Bassenwhaite to set up home and rear chicks of her own, kick-starting the whole cycle all over again.

Feeling happy and fulfilled with our encounter we left the Ospreys to enjoy their dinner in peace, and made our way back down the hill. As the sun set, flooding the valley with a mellow, deep golden

An azure damselfly.

glow, we had one last stop: the lake itself. We learnt that the church, white as a snowdrop, was named after St. Bega – I guess that's where our chick had got her name. We sat at the side of the lake with an ice cream each, watching the sun melt into the horizon; turning from gold to deep blood orange, streaked with pink and baby blue. Something tickled my hand, and looking down I saw one of the prettiest and most vividly coloured insects I had ever seen; an azure damselfly. True to their name, they are a vibrant, electric blue, their skinny abdomen banded with black. Extremely common, you normally see these beside bodies of water in the summer months either zig-zagging across the surface or settled on a stem or amongst the grass. This male was resting right beside my hand, and carefully I bent down to inspect his handsome markings. His wings were paper thin, delicate as glass and criss-crossed with tiny cells; his eyes were round and bulbous. Damselflies can appear similar to the fiercer sounding dragonfly, but there are a few differences to tell them apart. The forewings of dragonflies tend to be much bigger than the hindwings and at rest are held out to the side, like a plane. In damsels, they're around the same size and will be pressed together behind the insect, held vertically. Dragonflies are generally larger in size whereas damselflies tend to be slight and narrow – much like the dragons and damsels of fairy tales.

I leaned back onto my elbows. The damselfly, startled, burst up and hopped a little further away, where it settled once more and folded its wings carefully, like a person closing their favourite book. Amongst the grass he stood out like a sapphire, bright and glinting in the last of the daylight. As the moon appeared and twilight set in, we reflected on the magical experiences we'd had, returning home cheerful but sleepy having encountered dragons and frightened damsels all in one day.

Rutland Water, Leicestershire.

For those who seek ospreys ...

Scotland is the main stronghold for ospreys in the UK, but thanks to extensive conservation efforts there are now some great places in England where you can find them, too.

* **Rutland Water, Leicestershire:** this is an iconic site – the first where ospreys bred in England following a 150 year absence. Since then, Rutland has seen over a hundred chicks fledged.

* **Foulshaw Moss nature reserve, Cumbria:** Situated on the Kent estuary, Foulshaw Moss has a variety of aquatic habitat, from lakes to tarns. It is a popular stop-off for migrating ospreys as they travel to and from their winter grounds in West Africa.

* **Loch of Lowes (Dunkeld):** Set against a stunning backdrop of rolling hills and snow-capped peaks, catch sight of ospreys hunting in the glassy loch, where they have been nesting for almost 50 years.

* **Loch Garten (Aviemore):** One of the most beautiful settings in which to see these dramatic birds. Try and find red squirrels hiding in the surrounding Caledonian pine forest.

And if you're not feeling too adventurous, the majority of these reserves have live webcams on nests during breeding season, so you can monitor the chicks from the comfort of your couch, although I would always strongly suggest that you experience them in the great outdoors as well!. The Lake District Osprey Project, Loch of the Lowes and Loch Garten all provide links to nest-cams on their sites.

INLAND HABITATS

This chapter is for the wildlife not always found near water. Those who favour a slightly gentler habitat over wind-torn coastline, and prefer to build their homes amongst the boughs of trees as opposed to the squelchy banks of a river (I've heard these are prone to flooding and are only for those with a fantastic insurance policy).

Here in Britain, we have a vast diversity of 'inland' habitats that support a whole different subset of animals. Our woodlands, for instance, are home to a multitude of birds, insects and mammals, all to be found stalking the undergrowth for prey, nesting in tree trunks or foraging amongst the branches. Some animals we can all recognise, being popular characters from our childhood stories – badgers, squirrels, owls, hedgehogs, stoats and weasels. But delve deeper, and there is even more to be found. Take the oak tree, for example. A prominent feature of our countryside, they are regarded as the most biodiverse species of all our native trees and are home to more wildlife than any other. From the birds that nest within the depths of its trunk to the hundreds of spiders, beetles and other creepy-crawlies that scurry across the bark or hunt amongst the leaf litter. And of course, there are different types of woodland, each one with its own unique community of animal life. The mixed broadleaf typical to lowland areas; the dense pine forests of the uplands and the magical, ancient woodlands ... and everything in between.

Inevitably, the dark depths of these forests will open up and reveal even more natural wonders. Open grasslands are ideal places to spot deer, who once startled will seemingly dance across it in a graceful escape. Even our old agricultural land, with their overgrown pastures and crumbling farmhouses, are wildlife havens. Bats and small birds make use of derelict barns and buildings, roosting in the eaves and cavernous wall spaces and feasting on the insects that hover amongst the grasses and hedgerows. In summer, the meadows come to life; buttercups, poppies, daisies, cow parsley, and other wildflowers and herbs explode into colour in late spring, injecting bursts of scarlet, golden yellow, violet and white into the landscape. And these attract a great variety of butterflies and moths who flutter delicately about the meadow on painted wings. Another habitat that is important for

The views of Bennachie, Aberdeenshire.

insects is heathland – something that I'm very familiar with, living in Scotland – thick, spongey carpets of small shrubs, peppered with the mauve and lavender flowers of heather and little pops of bright yellow gorse. A diverse array of butterflies, dragonflies, moths and bees enjoy the bulbous flowers, whilst grasshoppers sing from the ground and enormous beetles bulldozer their way along the rocky paths. There are reptiles, too; adders hide and hiss in the bracken, and common lizards bask in rare patches of sunlight. And the patches of dense shrubs provide ideal cover for ground nesting birds. Here, you might find curlew, black grouse, nightjars, meadow pipits and even birds of prey – in particular the infamous hen harrier.

Whilst some of our most important environments, they are also our most threatened. These places are susceptible to human development, and many have been destroyed in favour of intensified agriculture or other kinds of land-use. Our woodlands, once extensive, have been shrunk to small patches dotted around towns and cities. British wildflower meadows are scarce, and heavy grazing by farming livestock has decimated most of our native grassland ... and some even say that heather moorland is rarer than rainforest. And the wildlife is suffering for it. Farmland birds, ground nesting birds and some species of bat are in decline, not to mention the insects who are vitally important for the health of the planet, like pollinators. Now more than ever, it's essential to go and visit these places and discover the wild things that are living there – before it's too late.

Glenmuick: The ideal place for a stag do

I f, like me, you are a wildlife enthusiast and/or an outdoors fanatic, it is important to have great adventure buddies (although honestly, I think this rule applies in general life). These are the people who accompany you on all your weird and wonderful adventures; those with which to while away the long, tedious car journeys and penguin-huddle behind a boulder when the weather turns on a walk. They are the people who heave you out of whatever bog you fell in, who give you a boost over a wall you're stuck on, and with who you share healthy doses of laughter and tea (... maybe something a little stronger if the situation demands) whilst thawing out in your tent or bothy. I am lucky to have not one of these adventure buddies, but several.

In my experience, these friends have awesome qualities that make them such good travel companions. For one, they remain resolutely cheery in the face of adversity – shrugging off gale-force winds and torrential, monsoon-style rain as 'a shower', for example. That person who says repeatedly in an overly cheerful tone 'we are not lost' when you've just passed the same landmark for the third time (or was it the fourth?). Also, they possess the most important quality – being able to put up with you and all your wildlife loving madness. They will successfully mask their frustration as you stop, yet again, to inspect or photograph yet another creature. And they will listen patiently, with a perfectly crafted expression of interest, as you wax lyrical about its many features and 'interesting' qualities. Even better, they might share in your passion and be genuinely excited, planning wildlife encounters with you and maybe even producing a value-pack of biscuits when beginning a long stake-out in a hide.

As detailed in the very pages of this book, many of the wildlife encounters I've had occurred in good company, and were all the better for it. The best times have been spent with these people, memories filled with the sound of laughter and food crackling over the fire; warm and vibrant, like summer caught in a jar. We made quite the team – every single one of us had some sort of skill to bring to the table, be it the navigational skills of a homing pigeon or the mountaineering skills of a goat. One has the culinary repertoire of a Michelin-starred chef, whipping up gourmet feasts of excellence over a camping stove. Another can pinpoint bird calls from a mile off, whilst another has the all-important entertainment factor and an

*Lochnagar,
Cairngorms
National Park.*

extensive suite of games to keep us going well into the night. There are those of us who can build a solid fire and get it roaring in seconds, and those who are always ridiculously upbeat and drag up the group morale, bouncing along ahead when the going gets tough. I have seen so much with this mad jumble of adventure seekers, and nothing gives me more pleasure than to remember these experiences for you.

One such adventure began with a conversation about socks. We were in the pub – as always, the best plans are always hatched in some sort of drinking establishment – and one of my friends was talking enthusiastically about his new pair of hiking socks. He is that type, the type to get endearingly excited about the most mundane of camping gear and who can quite happily while away the hours spoon whittling. It was then suggested that we all go on a trip to test out said socks and "get away from the city" – our favourite excuse – and began furiously googling places. One of us stumbled across a bothy that was owned by the university, situated in the North-east corner of the Cairngorms National Park. It was firmly announced as 'perfect' and The Plan was forged. We'd leave tomorrow after lectures!

The fact that it was mid-November and close to freezing temperatures did not cross our minds, an unfortunate consequence of beer and too many uni assignments.

The Cairngorms National Park is, currently, the biggest of its

kind in the British Isles. Look on the map, and it is a vast patch of rugged 'wilderness' towards the North-east of the country, a daunting but beautiful beast that incorporates the mountain range of its namesake and is filled with a rich mixture of habitats. Great, glassy black lochs reside in valleys, surrounded by formidable, towering hills and munros – mountains that are at least 3,000 feet high - that glower down over the surface of the water. Rivers tear through landscapes coloured mauve and cinnamon brown by heather, and there are pockets of ancient forest, filled with gnarly old trees and towering Caledonian pine. The Cairngorms can provide some of the most breath-taking views, the kind that make the steep, boggy climbs more than worth it. And it houses some of Scotland's most iconic wildlife, from the magnificent golden eagle that circles above the Douglas firs and Scot's pine, to the distinctly portlier and jester-like grouse that bumble away from you, chuckling their alarm call and looking like a living whisky advertisement. Capercaillie, pompous and forever-agitated birds, strut about looking for a fight. During breeding season, the males fan out their tails and fluff up the feathers about their neck causing them to look like some sort of hacked-off Elizabethan prince, the whole look topped off with a set of angry red eyebrows. Up on the snow-capped peaks, you might catch sight of ghost-like mountain hares or something that looks like an obese dove, otherwise known as a ptarmigan. Down below, the lochs are teeming with salmon and trout, attracting ospreys and otters; the woods hide red squirrels and pine martens that scamper around tree trunks with lightning speed. If you're especially lucky, you might even capture a glimpse of that elusive enigma, the Scottish wildcat. These striking animals are now rarer than Bengal tigers, to the extent that there is debate over whether true wildcats still exist in the wild. The problem is that they have bred with domestic cats, dissolving their heritage and producing hybrids that are hard to tell apart. I for one have never seen one, although every time I visit I say a little prayer to Mother Nature that I might be lucky.

It was both the wildlife and the promise of wide, open space that coaxed us from the city that following evening, with some nursing hangovers and others tired from lectures. We piled ourselves and our hastily packed gear into two cars and set out on the road. Our destination was just over ninety minutes' drive away to a place called Glenmuick, which is situated just outside Ballater within Balmoral estate. Nestled amongst rolling hills and thick patches of pine forest, the valley has more than one royal stamp of approval, having been immortalised in Lord Byron's poetry. Specifically, the poem refers to Lochnagar – the infamous munro that towers over the valley, often shrouded by mist and clouds which lends it a very dark and foreboding presence. One line is particularly apt to our trip: 'Round Lochnagar while the stormy mist gathers, winter presides in his cold icy car.' Being mid-November it was certainly cold and icy, and we shivered as we stepped outside our cars into darkness. There were two things we had not thought about whilst planning in the (very warm and cosy) pub: firstly, that in winter the sun sets at around four in the afternoon and secondly, the bothy was fairly far away from the car park. Having set off at three and stopping off at Morrisons for supplies, we had managed to arrive in pitch-darkness. The bothy is actually a twenty-minute walk down rough track, which can seem much longer when you can't see where you're heading and have gone a bit overboard on provisions.

But once over the initial shock of the biting cold and wishing that we'd decided against the extra jar of pasta sauce, the walk was magical. For me, a true measure of how rural an area is can be found by looking at the night sky. In Aberdeen, the dim orange glow of light pollution hangs over the city and only a few measly stars have struggled to make an appearance, like fireflies which have seemingly lost their way home. However, the night sky over the Cairngorms is a perfect velvety black with a whole smattering of stars; the air has that crystal-cut quality to it that makes everything seem crisp, clear

and miraculously still. Twice on that walk we heard the eerie hoot of a tawny owl gliding past, and the odd cackling sound of a male pheasant somewhere in the distance.

Once installed in the bothy (which, cruelly, is right behind a much fancier looking hunting lodge) we lit the fire, wolfed down some pasta and promptly fell asleep, with Glenmuick still engulfed in darkness. But with the next morning came the big reveal; the view. And my, what a view. A vast expanse of grassland leading up to Loch Muich lying calm and still, and the hills rising up to the sky. On a sunny day, the loch twinkles sapphire blue and the lands are tinged gold ... but on our first day we were threatened with a fine rain that seemed almost permanent and the hills were crowned in a fog so dense half of them were barely visible. Naturally, we chose this day to scale the Munro. As I said, all the good adventure buddies are the ones who make the least favourable of conditions enjoyable. That day we were all sodden from the off, slipping over wet stones and beaten by a vicious, icy wind that seemed to get worse the higher we climbed. Much wiser than us, very little wildlife seemed to have ventured out. Any animals we did see were given an eerie, ghostly look by the layers of mist and fog. A black grouse, his plumage furred with water droplets, sat with his back to us on a ledge overlooking the valley, the fine drizzle forming a sort of halo around his form. He made for a rather melancholy sight, his feathers sodden, his back hunched against the wind as he looked out over the ledge, contemplating the bad weather. We saw a few other grouse along the way, their white-ringed eyes starkly visible amongst the grey landscape about them. As we approached they would flush out from the heather in a great flurry of wings, chucking their indignation.

The view of Loch Muich and the rolling hills from our bothy door.

Melancholy red grouse braving the rain.

The higher we climbed, the thicker the mist became. The path in front of us became increasingly mysterious, only revealing itself as we advanced. Several mountain hares appeared to materialise suddenly out of the mist, only to vanish rapidly back into the undergrowth at the side of the path. They had their winter coats on, having exchanged their usual beige uniform for one of white, the only feature retained being the black tips on their ears. Somewhere halfway up we heard the familiar mewling call of a buzzard. Later, she came into sight, circling overhead in search of a potential snack. Buzzards are our most common bird of prey, which I think puts them at a slight disadvantage; they don't receive as much attention as their more 'iconic' cousins, the eagles, or the smaller and prettier red kite. But they are just as beautiful. A large bird, they are easy to identify from below due to a very distinctive white banding pattern on the underside of the wing and a slightly rounded tail. Close-up, they have a relatively small and delicately featured face in comparison to other raptors that I think has a distinctly feminine edge to it.

After the buzzard, the chance of seeing any other forms of wildlife was lost. The fog turned into relentless, driving sleet and the wind increased in strength from annoying to downright unmanageable. We were nearing the summit and about to approach the slightly vertigo-inducing ridge, which of course we were now blind to. A personal favourite quote of mine from the trip came from my good adventure buddy and chief navigator Tom, who warned us to not "stray too far from the path. Or if you do, give us a good scream so we know you've fallen off." The fact that he had to yell this to make himself heard over the howling wind made everything seem slightly more dramatic and had the effect of herding us into single file, not wanting to step one toe off the track.

Having miraculously avoided death and navigated the ridge, we made our way back down through the valley, frozen solid but exhilarated. The scenery around us was stunning. Shades of lavender and deep violet mixed in with little pops of green from the heather; the russet brown of the bracken broken by a river cascading through it. Waterfalls pounded over rocky overhangs, and trees began to appear, old and gnarled and mottled with lichens. The hills started to rise up around us again, and soon the wind had died down to a barely audible whisper. It was here we heard an odd sound; a deep-throated, hoarse call that seemed to come from the very belly of an animal. Simultaneously we all ground to a halt and looked at one another, listening ... the sound came again, and again, like blasts on a foghorn. We followed it up to the top of one of the nearby hills where, standing proudly on top and roaring for all to hear, was an enormous stag. His head was thrown back so that the sound carried, his crown of antlers nearly brushing his back. We stood quietly, watching him bellowing out his superiority so that it echoed around the valley. Stags will do this during breeding season to announce their strength and prowess to any potential love rivals. The louder and deeper your roar, the more fearsome of a competitor you are seen to be. This guy was a red deer, the biggest and by far most impressive of all the six species you can find in the UK, and an animal synonymous with Scotland. They are our biggest land mammal, the males weighing up to a hefty 190kg and boast a magnificent pair of highly branched antlers. They are such impressive animals, always seeming to stand stoic and proud in their beautiful auburn coat.

The autumn and winter months are the best and most exciting time to go and see red deer, as it is the infamous rutting season. During these months, the stags will return to their hind (their main

A red deer stag using a hill as his stage.

A red deer stag.

lady) in her home range and form harems with other females. Like the grandest of sultans, they strut and defend their harem in the face of a potential love rival – which can lead to the most spectacular and fierce battles, known as 'ruts'. Glenmuick is almost famous for its red deer population, and we'd arrived just as the breeding season was ending. I was just lucky enough to catch a rut, right on our doorstep. The day we were due to leave, I rose early hoping to make the most of the stunning views and the sunshine, which up until that moment had evaded us. I sat cradling a mug of tea in my hands, enjoying the pale winter sun and watching a robin hop cheerfully about the picnic table in front, his scarlet chest practically glowing in the watery lemon light. It was then that two stags materialised on the plains before me and began to 'parallel walk', moving in a very odd, stilted way whilst adjacent to one another. This is a behaviour used to size one another up, the first step to assessing their opponent's strength against their own. Many animals have ways of measuring an opponent's abilities that doesn't involve an actual fight; it takes a lot of energy to attack, and there is always the risk of injury or even death. So behaviours like parallel walking allow males to compete with one another without the need for a physical fight. Stags will also 'roar' to do this, that deep, guttural sound we'd heard from the individual on the hill. The two I was watching began to do it with such vigour, I wondered if they'd wake my comrades, still sound asleep in their sleeping bags like a nest of dormice.

Inevitably, one deer will out-perform the other. But on the rare occasion that a dispute cannot be settled this way, a fight ensues. The two males roared at each other several times, their breath forming hot steam in the brisk November air. Apparently, they were on a par, because suddenly one lowered his head, all muscles tensed in preparation for battle. I hardly dared believe my luck, half expecting the other to submit but instead he too dropped his antlers, and the two raced forwards and locked in battle. It was a fierce fight, their weaponry clacking loudly as they met and heads twisting this way and that, attempting to throw their opponent off balance. You could see the muscles ripple as they tried to drive each other backward, breathing heavily through their nostrils. Occasionally they would come to a standstill with antlers and eyes locked, legs splayed in a more secure stance, and I would wait with bated breath to see if one would give in. But then they'd be off again, sometimes turning circles on the spot in a very strange looking dance. Evidently, they were quite evenly matched.

This ferocious war carried on for all of five very exciting minutes, during which time my tea turned cold and the robin vacated his perch, when finally, one male tired and gave up. Breaking contact he turned heel and skittered off in the other direction, leaving the victor to stand tall and strut behind him, snorting in derision with his chest puffed out. It was kind of like watching a fight between two bodybuilders at the gym — both filled with testosterone and machismo. For a time, the winner stood watching his adversary retreat and I got a good look at him. From the battle scars that adorned his nose and the decidedly greyish tinge to his coat, I estimated he was older and more seasoned in battle. I must have got quite into the drama because I felt almost relieved for him that he'd kept his seat, and raised my cold brew in acknowledgement.

Just at that moment, the bothy door opened – the male turned heel and fled into some nearby pine trees. It always surprises me how even something as powerful and regal as a stag can be startled at the smallest thing. I'd always imagined stags to find courage in those enormous antlers, yet we could only approach within 50 yards before the bravest would turn and flee. I looked up and found my friend smiling down with an offering of a hot cup of

When and where to see red deer rut

When...
* Autumn, more specifically October – the first two weeks are prime rutting season.
* Rutting activity is at its most intense in the three hours after dawn, when resident males are seeing off newcomers that have arrived in the night. Just before dusk is a good time, too.
* This means a very early start or potentially a late finish … but it's more than worth it! Rutting is one of our most exciting wildlife spectacles.

Where...
Woodlands, country estates, and public parks are the best places to seek them out. Here are a few of the best:
* **Cairngorms national park:** there are multiple places here to witness deer. You can take a guided tour of the Braes of Glenlivet to see the rutting stags of Kymah burn. If you're lucky, you might even see a golden eagle along the way, too.

* **Isle of Arran and Isle of Jura:** Both islands have huge populations of deer (on Jura humans are outnumbered 30 to 1) so you have a great chance of finding them here.

* **Fountains Abbey and Studley Royal park, North Yorkshire:** This deer park, where 500 individuals roam free, has a specific 'deer walk' mapped out for visitors to guarantee.

* **Exmoor National Park:** Not just for red deer, you also have chance of spotting fallow and roe. If you're feeling particularly fancy you can treat yourself to a '4x4 safari' which takes you right to the heart of the action.

* **Richmond park, Greater London:** A little less wild, but surprisingly one of the best locations to photograph red deer as they move through the trees.

* **Foulshaw Moss, Cumbria:** Stags often rut out in the middle of this lowland peat bog, making them easy to see.

tea and a biscuit; as I said, these are some of the most important qualities in an adventure buddy, especially as my bum and fingers were suitably numbed from sitting on the concrete. Apparently, they had all been watching through the window from indoors the whole time and in exhilarated tones we relived the experience over breakfast. Some of these experiences are like a great cake: best shared with friends.

On our way back to the car, I found the aftermath of that fight – an antler, still warm and bloodied. It now stands pride of place in my office, a reminder of one of my favourite places in the world and good times spent with buddies.

Stag in Glen Rosa - Isle of Arran - Scotland.

Tips ... Approach downwind and try to conceal yourself in vegetation. Deer are flighty – even those with impressive weaponry – and are easily scared away. Tread quietly, and listen out for stags roaring, as this precedes the main event..

The ghost of the moors

Heather moorland is one of our most iconic landscapes. Rolling hills speckled purple by heather and shrouded in mist; scenes filled with drama and intrigue that have provided the setting for many a literary masterpiece. But aside from being the dramatic back-drop to wandering about clad in a frilly nightie and searching for Heathcliff, our moors have so many other reasons for being important – not just nationally, but internationally. Staggeringly, over 70 per cent of the word's heather moorland is found right here, in Britain. A significant proportion of this is in the uplands of Scotland, and the undulating landscapes of lilac and olive-brown have become associated with scenery north of the border. Heathland looks particularly melodramatic under stormy skies; something which Scotland has a bountiful supply of.

On the surface, it may seem that these endless hills are barren and inhospitable. Wind battered, exposed to the wet and cold, they offer very little tree cover and feature rocky patches and boulders – you could be excused for imagining nothing would really want to

Heather up-close.   *A scotch argus butterfly.*

hang around much. Heather is a low-lying shrub, and when looking at it from a distance it can appear like there is nothing much to see. But when managed properly and sympathetically, moorland can be rich in animal and plant-life. It is not just one habitat, but several, all jumbled together in a biodiverse patchwork quilt of nature. Each little patch contains its own pick 'n' mix of species, all of which knit together to create a functioning ecosystem – heather moorland is certainly not 'just heather'.

My research focussed on birds of prey, and I've spent much of the last few years hiking in the uplands. Many species love the variety of food available in these habitats, from golden eagles who nest in the trees that fringe the moors to buzzards, wheeling overhead and crying out in mewling voices. Spending such a significant amount of time here, I could fully appreciate what made each habitat special. And as spotting raptors often means extended periods of sitting (and a healthy dose of patience), I've had ample opportunity to watch wildlife come and go. Battling up through dry heath up to my waist and stumbling into ditches of wet heath, dotted with the spikey, sulphur-yellow flowers of bog asphodel, I've walked in the wake of butterflies and moths as they dance over the woody shrubs. Fritillaries are always present, including the scotch argus – a beautiful, delicate butterfly with brown velvet wings, bordered in orange and white. There are great, gloriously fuzzy emperor moths, who sometimes need rescuing from puddles in wet weather; and delicate, pretty moths with jazzy patterns, like the lovely-named 'true lover's knot'.

The heather itself is alive with sound. The buzzing of bees as they go about collecting pollen, hopping between the little purple buds, or the brief, shrill shout of a meadow pipit next to the more twee, bleating call of a golden plover. Heather moorland is the ideal habitat for ground-nesting birds such as these. The dense shrubs conceal their nests and young, but are also beside areas of shorter vegetation in which to find food. One of the most sought-after of these birds is the ring ouzel, or 'mountain blackbird'. A member of the thrush family, they are related to their more common garden cousins and have a similar diet of insects, berries and worms. But they are smaller and slighter with a longer tail, and a distinctive white band around the breast. I've only seen one of these – a male, who landed right in front of me during a stake-out to catch sight of peregrines. He seemed to not notice me for some time, and busied himself pecking at fallen bilberries that had scattered on the ground like spilled sweets. But when he did eventually realise he was not alone he seemed horrified, fixing me with a beady-eyed stare and ostensibly rooted to the spot. In respect (it can be quite embarrassing to realise you've made an error), I didn't move an inch until he worked up the courage to flit away.

I've seen such a variety of animals and plants on moorland that I never leave disappointed, even if the bird of prey in question doesn't show. But there is one experience that I will never forget, and it all happened in the space of one weekend.

Throughout my PhD I saw many birds of prey, but there was one that always evaded me – the hen harrier. This is mostly down to the fact that harriers are our most threatened raptor, mainly due to extensive illegal killing that occurs in parts of the country (extremely sad and a point I will come to later) but also – to a lesser extent – habitat loss and predation. Hen harriers are decidedly picky about their choice of home and have a number of preferences: clumpy heather in which to nest, interspersed with more open land in which to hunt, which makes them susceptible to change. Coming into the last year of my PhD still having never seen one, I made it my mission to observe them in the wild before the year was out. I have a bucket list of species I want to see, and several birds of prey species are on there – many of which I've ticked off and the encounters detailed in this book. But the hen harrier was a resounding absence. Luckily, the nature of my work means I get to speak to some of the best raptor workers in the country, and three agreed to take me out onto the moors and show me 'their' harriers with an almost guaranteed success rate. And so,

I set out on a drizzly Friday morning in June filled with optimism, hope and an enormous packet of biscuits (hobnobs will forever be the biscuit of choice, in case you're wondering).

We began our journey in pine forest, our footsteps muffled by a thick blanket of old needles coloured rusty red and the air thick with the scent of sap and warm foliage. The weather was feeling indecisive that day, and short bursts of rain would be broken by golden floods of sunlight, which filtered through the canopy to form dappled patterns on the path. As we picked our way over sprawling fingers of tree root and fallen logs, a cuckoo sounded his bright and cheerful call. I never tire of this sound; it reminds me of the cuckoo clock which hangs on the wall in my parents' house, its merry chime announcing the turn of every hour. I used to be fascinated by the little, jointed wooden bird, which would bow jerkily with every 'cuckoo'. The actual recording in the clock came from a forest in Switzerland, and you can even hear the babbling of a brook in the background and the echo reverberating around the empty ranks of trees. It's odd to be in the depths of a forest and hear that sound in 'real life' – especially as cuckoos are quite difficult to spot. It can be easy to imagine the sound is just coming from a clock nailed to a tree. But this time, I saw the owner of that call as we rounded a corner and came to a clearing. The cuckoo is a medium sized bird, grey in colour with a distinctive banding pattern across the chest. It is thought that the adult colouring is meant to mimic that of a more fearsome bird – a sparrow hawk – which fools other birds and gives the female time to lay her eggs unnoticed. Cuckoos are masters of deception. Not only do they mimic other birds, but they are 'brood parasites'; laying their eggs in another birds' nest, most often those of dunnocks and meadow pipits. The eggs are perfectly crafted to look like those of the host bird, so as not to arouse suspicion – and it works. The female will simply wait for the opportune moment before flying down, cheekily pushing one egg out of the host nest and replacing it with her own. She then calmly flies off, leaving some other poor soul to shoulder the burden. It's the perfect crime; she ensures her genes are passed on without bearing any of the hardships of parenting. Perhaps the worst (but in a sadistic way, the most comedic) part of this is that the cuckoo offspring quickly becomes much bigger than its bewildered adoptive parents, who feed its insatiable appetite with admirable commitment.

Shortly after the cuckoo flew across our path, the forest opened into an extensive landscape of gentle valleys and low hills, a watercolour of deep mauve, green and red-brown blending into one another. To climb the hill and get to our 'viewing point', we first had

Cuckoo.

to dip down into the valley and cross a burn (a small stream), which as you can imagine was the wettest place and mostly made up of blanket bog. Bogs are the most deliciously messy of all habitats and provide opportunity as an adult to return to childhood, when you used to get as muddy and wet as possible (much to the annoyance of your parents). It can be super fun to splash and squelch your way across the bog – well, if you have decent boots on. At that time my boots were slightly leaky (my better, waterproof pair had succumbed to mould and spiders in Madagascar a few months previously) and as such, I spent the rest of the day with soggy feet. I did try to pick my way across using grassy tussocks as stepping stones, with some degree of success. Bogs are characterised by the delightfully oozy and absorbent sphagnum moss (otherwise known as the 'bog-roll' of the wild – try it if you're caught short) and long grasses, such as deer grass and bog cotton. The latter has little, snow-white balls of fluff-like stuff at the top of the stem, which sway faintly in the wind and look like a big group of dancing rabbits. Some of these grasses and mosses form little clumps, allowing you to hop from one to the other. But losing your footing can be disastrous, bringing you splashing down into a glutinous mud up to your knees. I did realise, however, that falling over in bogs can be a great wildlife-spotting technique, for it was during one of the times that I discovered a meadow pipit

Meadow pipit nest.

nest. I noticed the small, round entrance from my new horizontal viewpoint, carefully tucked away in the long grass. Ever so gently I brushed away the fronds of bog cotton that partially concealed it, and from inside two pairs of bright, sharp eyes looked back at me. Two chicks, sitting plump and ruffled in the warmth of their hiding place, blinked back in surprise. They must have been fairly old, as their downy feathers had already taken on the dashed brown and pale-yellow pattern of an adult bird. Yet their wide, stubby beaks looked too big for them, and they were still decidedly fluffy. I looked up towards the sky, but I could not hear or see a parent; presumably they'd gone out in search of some tasty insects with which to feed their brood. Luckily for said parents, there was no sign of a cuckoo-shaped intruder...

After jumping the burn, bog turned into wet heath, with its mixture of cross-leaved heath, sedges and rushes. Here is the land of the amphibians and reptiles. As we walked, a common frog hopped frantically away from us, pausing as we did and gulping hastily, eyes bulging. A common lizard basked in one of the rare patches of sunlight, legs splayed for maximum effect and eyes closed in sheer enjoyment. These lizards are a murky brown colour with a distinctive dark band that runs behind the eye and down the flanks, and can be found regulating their body heat when the moment arises, be it on rocks, logs or furry humps of grass. And amongst the heather, adders lurked; easily distinguishable due to the contrasting 'zig-zag' pattern of black and olive green that runs along the length of their body, coiled into loops like a jazzy pile of rope. As we climbed higher, we followed a rough, stony path which snaked up around the valley, now keeping our eyes peeled for harriers while around us the meadow pipits danced and dived.

Finally, we arrived at our destination, an area of dense, dry heath, perfectly situated to look upon the valley beneath where the harriers liked to feed, and a rocky outcrop, the bottom of which was the suspected nest site. We settled in for a long stay – catching sight of a hen harrier could take up to three hours. However, it was quite comfortable. The mixture of heather and sponge-like sphagnum

Our harrier viewing point.

moss makes for a well-cushioned seat, especially when combined with a flask of something hot and a hobnob or two to nibble on. Watching and waiting for wildlife isn't everyone's cup of tea, but for some it can be extremely peaceful; just you, the sky and the wind whispering through the vegetation around you. Especially up on the moors, where quite often there doesn't seem to be another person for miles. Instead we were surrounded by bell and common heather and the sounds of the bees as they busied themselves with more important tasks. One species unique to moorland has my favourite bee-name ever; the bilberry bumble bee. These bees are characterised by a bright orange abdomen, and as the name suggests they prefer the flowers of the bilberry shrub. Bilberries look much like the blueberries you can pick up in the supermarket, little denim blue berries that release deep purple juices when crushed. They are important food sources for many animals of the moor, including deer picking their way through the hills, nibbling incessantly and stopping every now and again, mid-chew, to scan for danger. On the hill across from us, a few fallow deer made their way across the moor at a leisurely pace, nipping berries from the shrubs as they went and pausing whenever they found a particularly good patch. These deer are very pretty animals, usually a shade of tan or fawn, with dainty white spots along the back and a white horseshoe on the rump. Their hearing is impeccable; if one of us shifted our weight ever so slightly, the deer would look up in alarm with ears pricked, frozen with muscles tensed, ready for a quick getaway.

The most common colouring of fallow deer is the one I described earlier, but as we sat a pair appeared that confused us. One was the typical 'Bambi' style I was accustomed to, but the other was a deep, chocolate brown with no spotting whatsoever. We squinted at them repeatedly through the binoculars wondering if this was some sort of inter-species friendship, although not one of us had ever seen a deer that colour. Later, frantic googling told us it was in fact the much rarer melanistic variety; still a fallow deer, but just one with a genetic variation that meant more of the darker pigment, melanin, was produced, much like skin pigmentation in humans. This discussion, coupled with the huge variety of other wildlife, kept us entertained in the hours we waited for the bird that we had actually come to find.

Searching for a specific animal is truly an exercise in patience and perseverance. As time rolls on, you begin to see and hear things – a blob on the horizon the exact colour and form of your subject just turns out to be a conveniently shaped rock, or that noise you are convinced is the animal's call is simply the wind screeching around the corner. We had a few red herrings of our own that day; some

ravens nesting on a rocky outcrop nearby were using the wind to glide, in such a way that they looked like a harrier silhouetted against the sky. It was their loud, raspy squawk that gave the game away. A kestrel, hovering and dive-bombing the heather around us only became a kestrel on closer inspection, which revealed its speckled red and grey colouring. Three times I got unnecessarily excited by him, until the experts informed me that extended hovering was in fact a very un-harrier like behaviour, reserved only for the smaller falcons. We became so used to this cycle of excitement, realisation and disappointment that we almost missed the star of the show. I wouldn't have spotted him had I not been reaching round to offer the team a biscuit (see? Hobnobs are great things to take on these kinds of excursions).

Finally – almost three hours in – a male harrier shot up from the undergrowth behind us, so starkly light in colour that he was hard not to identify, standing out like a ghost against the purple of the heather. His wings were held high behind him, so we could see the jet-black tips of his wings, and his gaze was intensely focussed at the heather below. A mixture of pale grey and white, he was like a remnant of winter in the depths of summer. But he disappeared as suddenly as he'd arrived, vanishing down into the other valley behind us – we'd been staring at the wrong place the whole time! Hastily,

A far-away fallow deer on the look out.

Hen Harrier.

we gathered up our things and high-tailed it over to the next valley, not even bothering to leap across the bogs we encountered. I was so excited, I barely noticed the small puddles forming inside my boots.

The next valley was much steeper with a small loch cradled in the middle, and here we had much better luck. Almost as soon as we had set up camp the male – or a male at least – appeared, much further away but so easy to follow, standing out like a snowflake amongst a sea of green. Wings outstretched, he glided effortlessly up the adjacent side of the valley, crossing a burn and turning back on himself. At this time of year, the hen harriers would have made a nesting attempt, and raptor workers across the country would be praying for success – and chicks. We were looking out for tell-tale signs of parenthood; hunting, and a behaviour called a 'food pass' where the male would deliver any prey he had caught to the female, mid-air. However, this male began to do something very unusual and worrying. He made his way up to the top of the hill, a white dot becoming smaller and smaller still. And then he began to dance, soaring skywards before plunging back down, over and over again, in a dramatic display of aerial acrobatics. This, I knew, was called skydancing – the harriers' breeding behaviour. Usually performed in spring, it is an awe-inspiring spectacle where the male 'dances' for the female's attentions. But at this time of year it carries a worrying undercurrent; it could mean the nest had failed, for reasons unknown to us, and the male was therefore trying again. It was still breath-taking to watch - even as I squinted intently from my far-away perch, like a pauper in the cheap seats at an opera. We watched as the white spot bounced along the skyline, like a ping-pong ball, before it vanished out of sight behind the hill.

For a brief moment, there was murmurings of a nest failure and furrowed brows about our group. But then another flash of white grabbed our attention – this time much closer. Another male hen harrier! Like a ghost he appeared out of nowhere, and from the opposite direction to the last. We all agreed it must be a different individual; no bird could move that fast, no matter how skilled or streamlined. And then we witnessed the piece de resistance, the behaviour we all hoped we'd see – a food pass. Deftly, he soared across the landscape with something small clutched in both talons and emitting a curious, chattering sound. He was calling to the female, the harrier signal for "dinner's ready!". Almost immediately she came hurtling around the corner of a rocky outcrop to our right, her plumage a more demure, mottled brown, blending in to the muted colours of the hills. The pair flew right at each other as if they might collide; then, at the very last minute, both drew up and hovered with astonishing accuracy. In a matter of seconds, the little parcel of food had been passed between them. Promptly both wheeled about and flew off in opposite directions; she presumably back to the nest, he back out to hunt once more. This was the best news we could have received. A food pass meant the harriers had nested, and more importantly, had been successful – there were chicks on the nest. With the hen harrier as rare as it is, it really lifted my heart to know that at least somewhere, the new generation was being welcomed into the world.

The following day, fully equipped with dry socks and (semi-dry) boots, we set off to a different site to visit an active nest, where it was suspected by my colleague that chicks had hatched a few weeks ago and therefore should be big enough to cope with a visit. As a monitor of such a rare bird, nest visits are an unfortunate but necessary part of the job. However, so much effort must be put in to minimise disturbance as much as possible – our team was reduced to two, and we were only allowed a maximum of twenty minutes in which to find and record the nest. I felt extremely privileged to have been asked along, and also hoping that the tracking skills I'd amassed when working in Africa would hold up when put to the test.

This time there was no path, and we battled through waist-deep heather and squeezed through thickets of juvenile fir trees, coloured a vivid lime green and covered in young, rubbery needles. Scattered about the shrub were gloriously hairy caterpillars dressed in Beetlejuice colours, plump and bristling and almost ready to pupate. We climbed until my thighs started to ache and the sky coloured a threatening shade of charcoal, the clouds heavy with the weight of rain. But it wasn't long before we heard the female sounding her alarm call, a high-pitched squeal of sound that spoke of danger coming. I looked up and saw her circling overhead, seeing the cream patterns of her underside and the gentle taper of her wings. Immediately I felt like an intruder; twice she swept low over our heads, causing the taller of the two of us to have to stoop low so to avoid collision. Promptly we began an intense search, keen to minimise the amount of time the female was off the nest as much as possible.

It was like finding a needle in a haystack. The vegetation was in thick, irregular clumps and there were no landmarks to stick to, so often we ended up walking in circles. As we zig-zagged across the area we strained our ears for the chirping sound of chicks, but the meadow pipits were panicking too, and being more numerous were extremely loud. This, coupled with the rain that had begun to fall in great, fat droplets and splatted off my hood, made it hard to hear anything. The only guide we had to go on was the female's behaviour, who seemingly got angrier the closer we were. It was like that childhood game, where you hide something and tell the searcher they're getting warmer or colder depending on their proximity to its hiding place.

After about fifteen minutes of intense searching, I stumbled across a nest crafted out of dry twigs and grass about the size of a dinner plate – and in it, sitting squat and slightly soggy, were two plump, fluffy chicks. They were covered in thick, fuzzy down and coloured a dull beige-grey, their canary yellow legs and beak a stark contrast. Already, their beaks had hardened and curved, the ends dipped in black. As we crouched down in the heather to meet them, I couldn't stop myself from smiling; few people get to see an adult hen harrier, let alone their offspring. They were also hugely comic in their enraged disapproval of our presence, glaring up at us with beady black eyes and wheezing indignantly in our faces. One was most certainly much bigger than the other and took the leading role, standing up over his sibling and shrieking incessantly. I sympathised; I would be more than a little annoyed if someone just walked into my flat unannounced, then decided to sit and stare rudely at me.

This was an incredibly special moment for me. Not just because hen harriers feature in my research, but also because the population has been severely threatened for such a long time. Scotland is labelled as a 'stronghold' for harriers, but there are far fewer individuals than there should be. And in England, sadly, there remains just a handful.

Two disgruntled hen harrier chicks in the nest.

Heather moorland is their preferred habitat, but is also the site chosen for the field sport of driven grouse shooting for which large proportions of heather are managed and maintained. Additionally, hen harriers will take some grouse chicks, mainly with which to feed their young during the brooding season, and this brings them into conflict with grouse moor management. In 1954, it was made illegal to kill, harm or disturb any bird of prey – but still, many individuals per year are shot or poisoned and the hen harrier is a prime focus of this. It's so disheartening. They should be a regular feature of our moors, and their absences speak volumes. Great, empty spaces exist where the 'ghost of the moors' should be gliding and the air filled with their curious, cackling call. So, to find a successful nest filled my heart with joy, and as I crouched there looking into two endearing, fluffy faces, I made a silent prayer that these two would lead long lives, unhampered by danger.

How to find harriers (responsibly)

A wee disclaimer here: I was fortunate enough to head out with professionals, who carry licences that allow them to visit nests and tag chicks. I was covered under these licences, but to disturb a nest without one is illegal. These birds are precious, and should not be disturbed except for research purposes – even then, measures are taken to ensure disturbance is minimal. Admire them from a distance, and if you find a nest leave it well alone.

That being said, there are still ways to enjoy seeing them:

* Find heather moorland with a mixed variety of habitat: thick shrub cover, but also open pasture where they like to hunt.

* Position yourself so you're looking down on the area. Sit still, and try not to wear bright clothing – neutral tones are best.

* The best time to see them is between March and August, during breeding season. Look out for characteristic behaviour, such as skydancing.

* The males are pale in colour and easy to see, but the females are brown – instead look out for their white rump spot and distinct banding on the tail, which lends them their nickname, 'ringtail'.

* Be patient: it can take hours to find a bird of prey. Raptor monitors are brilliant at perseverance!

* And finally … sightings are highly valued. If you see a bird, note down what it looked like, its behaviour (e.g. was it hunting? Nest building?) and if you can, a grid reference. These can then be reported to **RSPB's Hen Harrier Hotline**, where it will be used towards the conservation of this wonderful species.

Once the nest site and its inhabitants were recorded, we left the little family in peace. By now the female was very annoyed with us, shouting a series of high-pitched kek sounds and circling furiously above us. We made a hasty retreat and then, at a safe distance, looked over our shoulders. Thankfully, the female was nowhere to be seen, hopefully meaning she had settled back on the nest. Satisfied, we weaved our way back down through woodland just as the sun came out, heralded by cuckoos and the whiny cry of a buzzard. It had certainly been a magical few days and as I ticked 'hen harrier' from my list, I felt very lucky indeed.

Hen Harrier.

A species in the red

I f there was one species that encapsulated the nature of Britain's wildlife, it would be the red squirrel. Notoriously shy, elusive, and on its way to recovery following a troubled past. But for once, this is a species that was brought to extinction by another animal, instead of humans. Well, kind of.

Their nemesis is another species of squirrel – the grey, native to America but introduced to the UK in 1876. A Victorian banker (who now has an awful lot to answer for) brought a pair back and released them on his land, and they soon became a novelty. Other landowners followed suit, wanting a fancy foreign species for themselves – but of course, they couldn't have had any idea the trouble it would eventually cause. Grey squirrels carry a disease called parapoxvirus, or 'squirrel pox' as it is more commonly known. Whilst it is not deadly to them it is fatal to red squirrels, who die within two to three weeks of contracting it. Following the spread of these invasive aliens, the population of reds in England was soon decimated and they became an endangered species in serious need of help. And it wasn't just the virus, either. The grey squirrels in Scotland, for some reason, did not carry the virus, but still the reds suffered from their presence. They were outcompeted by these larger, stronger foreigners, who vied for the same food and shelter. For example, red squirrels can only eat ripe acorns; they are unable to digest the green ones. But greys – even though they can stomach the greener nuts – will beat them to it, devouring the stocks before reds have even had a look in. And when put under pressure, red squirrels will fail to breed – something that hasn't really helped their chances.

As a result, grey squirrels have replaced reds across almost all of England and Wales. Scotland, where the decline was slower, remains a stronghold with 75 per cent of the entire population residing there. But when you consider there are over 2.5 million grey squirrels and only 140,000 reds, the impact of their competition really hits home. Now, I'm making grey squirrels sound like a bit of a bully here. It's not exactly their fault – they are just a bigger, more successful species, and our wee natives just weren't ready for them. If you think about it, the grey squirrel has now been around for more than a century. Some people have grown quite attached; more have seen a grey squirrel in the wild than a red one, and as such the debate as to whether we should control the former is quite a contentious subject in some parts of the country. One of my good friends, Holly, works for the Red Squirrel Trust in Wales, and one of the more difficult parts of her job is introducing the concept of grey squirrel control to the locals who have fairly mixed feelings about it – the majority agree it's a necessity, but similarly have grown attached to the greys. But she also has the pretty great job of monitoring the other locals – the red squirrels – and she knows the best places to find them.

Holly covers the Bangor area, which includes northern Gwynedd, and Anglesey. Anglesey is one of the best examples of red squirrel conservation in the country; in 1997 the population numbered 40, but now, twenty years later, that number has risen to almost 800. It's a brilliant case study to illustrate just how well red squirrels can do in the absence of greys. Even now, in just a year they've spread to mainland Wales, recolonising areas from where they were once absent. I was excited to see the success for myself and headed down

Britannia bridge in Anglesey.

for a holiday in early autumn when I knew they'd be most active, frantically gathering food in preparation for the harsher months ahead.

Our site was one of Holly's favourites – a place called Coed Mor, a sheltered woodland beneath the Britannia bridge in Anglesey. It's a bit of an odd place for wildlife spotting, with the traffic of the A55 roaring overhead, but except for that, it's relatively quiet. Not many people go there, meaning the squirrels are left in peace and there's a much higher chance of seeing one. As I mentioned earlier, red squirrels are enormously shy. They hate disturbance of any kind and will avoid being on the forest floor at all costs, preferring to stay up high in the tree canopy. Despite mostly being a fiery shade of ginger, they are actually very well camouflaged and when feeling vulnerable will plaster themselves to the bark of a tree, becoming so still it's easy to mistake them for an autumn leaf. But this is where being in the company of an expert with insider knowledge really helps.

Coed Mor is not only peaceful, but is mostly a mixture of conifer and beech trees; apparently, squirrel heaven. We walked slowly through the woods, treading carefully so as not to make too much noise. It was a clear, still day; the autumn sun bright and sharp, illuminating the leaves as they began to turn golden. Our vantage point was a clearing that looked out across the Menai straits all the way to Bangor. The strait is a stretch of tidal water that separates Anglesey from the mainland – when we arrived, it was the height of high tide and the strait was swollen and glistening in the sun. In the middle of the strait lay a little white cottage, presumably on an island, but from our point of view it looked as though the building was floating on the surface of the water, seemingly weightless. The reason for being here was two-fold, as we were not only looking out for red squirrels, but also on grey watch. There are many access routes here for greys to get onto Anglesey from the mainland; the Menai bridge, the railway, and even the strait itself. I was surprised to learn that greys are competent swimmers and could transverse a body of water with ease in calm waters - although they avoid strong tidal currents. Luckily, that day we didn't come across any grey pioneers – but we did see lots of red squirrels, which I was extremely happy about!

Before visiting, I'd brushed up on my red squirrel knowledge. I knew to look out for signs of their presence in the woodland; scratch marks on trees, nibble marks on new pine cones and cone 'debris' on the forest floor, where the squirrel has torn off the spines to access the seeds (they look like a half-eaten corn on the cob). Apparently, you can even tell whether the individual is left or right handed, depending on the marks ... although I don't think I'm that much of an expert. Squirrels will also leave a 'notch' in the top of nuts, where they've bitten into the top to split it in half. But according to my companion, the best way to find red squirrels was to listen for them. We had the perfect day; still and beautifully silent, with not even

Red squirrel appearing from a feeder.

the faintest breeze to rattle the leaves. Mainly, we were listening for the dull thunk of beech nuts hitting the forest floor as the hungry foragers discarded them – apparently, squirrels have little in the way of table manners. You could also hear them scrabbling about the leaf litter or chucking to one another, having conversations as they worked, and making a racket as they crashed from tree to tree; it's surprising just how much noise such a small animal can make. On a tranquil day like ours, it was easy to follow the sound to its source, and we found a number of them this way.

If we were quiet enough, the squirrels wouldn't run away – at least not immediately. We were visiting them in peak food-gathering time when they were at their busiest and most frenetic, and least likely to notice intruders. Contrary to popular belief squirrels don't hibernate; instead, they cache food. Surplus nuts, seeds and fungi are collated throughout the year and stored in various locations about the forest: hidey-holes in the trunks of a tree, or buried underground. This method is known as 'scatter-hoarding', and is a bit like an insurance policy. If you've stored your treasured possessions in multiple different places, you'll always have one to fall back on if the other is ransacked.

Like all animals, no two individuals were the same. We saw a whole range of fur colours, from sandy orange to cinnamon red, chestnut brown to even patches of black. Similarly, some had ear tufts whereas others didn't. These tufts are one of the red squirrels' most characteristic features; little amber tussocks of fur that they use to communicate feelings, like a dog. They are one of the fool-proof ways to tell a red and a grey apart, as greys never possess them. Confusingly however, a lot of the red squirrels we saw that day didn't have any either. We'd arrived at that one time of year when the tufts were shed – but only briefly. They'd be regrown within a week or so, becoming most prominent during winter. Some individuals had faint wisps of hair just visible on top of their pointed ears, in an odd sort of frizzy hairstyle.

Even more confusing was the fact that some of them had tinges of grey. Squirrels moult twice a year, changing their coat from its warmer winter version to a cooler one in spring, and vice versa as the colder months arrive. This can give red squirrels the appearance of greys, and greys the appearance of reds. For example, we spotted an individual with a dappled grey body but red 'sleeves' where the shorter fur hadn't moulted. Consequently, the line between greys and reds can be somewhat blurred. Luckily that particular squirrel had ear tufts, but when these are lost too it can be a little perplexing. The best distinguishing feature to go by is the tail; in general, red

squirrel tails are all one colour, whereas the tail of greys is made up of many different shades. Additionally, the fur of the latter is fringed with white-tipped fur, giving it a 'halo' effect. Greys also tend to be beefier with stocky, rounded bodies; red squirrels are small and slight.

As well as aesthetics, the individuals we came across had varying personalities. Some were true to form; painfully shy, they would vanish back up into the canopy as we approached and we would see nothing but an auburn streak. Others, however, were a little more confident and would become quite annoyed at our presence. They would 'chatt' at us agitatedly - a sound not unlike the tisk of a

A squirrel chows down on a nut.

It can be hard to photograph squirrels as they dash up a tree, so excuse the shoddy camera work but you can see the varying colours of this individual. Red squirrels aren't just red!

blackbird – and stare anxiously down from their perches. Some would even become so riled that they would begin foot tapping, a behaviour displaying anger and unrest. On the other side of the spectrum were the squirrels who clearly had more important business to attend to. These ones would just flatly ignore us and continue to faff about, industriously gathering nuts or scrabbling about in the undergrowth. If you knelt low on the ground and sat quietly, you could hear them making a gentle squeaking sound, like guinea pigs. We watched them go about their busy lives for some time, marvelling the way they used their plump, bushy tails for balance whilst scampering along the skinniest of branches, or admiring their extreme cuteness as they paused to nibble at a nut. At these times, they would rest back on their haunches with their tail curled up behind them, like a cushion. Tiny, clawed hands would clutch onto the item and their eyes would glaze over. Whether this was because they were transfixed on the task ahead or down to sheer pleasure, we couldn't be certain. But for these brief moments they were completely still – something that is extremely rare for a squirrel – the only movement coming from their mouths as they chewed rapidly, noses twitching with the effort.

We spent a very enjoyable day in the company of squirrels. The woodland was indeed very quiet – no other human appeared all day, and it felt very special wandering the thickets of beech with nothing but the crunch of leaves underfoot and the distant thunder of the A55. Listening intently for the faintest evidence of our bushy-tailed friends, my other senses were heightened. The scents of the wood were more noticeable; the fresh sharpness of pine-sap and the rich, cloying scent of the earth. Sounds became clearer, twigs and branches crackling with our footsteps and the impertinent chirp of a brambling somewhere in the trees above us. I could feel the air warming ever so slightly as the day rolled on, the mild warmth on my skin whenever the canopy allowed the sun to break through. Holly found a drey – a squirrel nest – cradled in the fork of a tree, a largish ball of twigs and moss carefully crafted and hidden. It is illegal to look inside, but admiring from a distance we didn't see any activity; presumably, there was no-one home. Dreys are multi-purpose, serving as nests for young (squirrel babies are referred to as 'kittens', which is rather adorable), food stores and places to shelter when the weather turns bad. Inside, there may be nest material, big piles of beech nuts and little segments of fungi – a secret stash of winter goodies. I like to imagine red squirrels as the OCD mothers of the animal kingdom: fully prepared for any eventuality and fastidiously organised for those 'just in case' moments.

As we left the woods and its inhabitants behind, I wondered what the future of these little scarlet busybodies would be. Squirrelpox spreads like wildfire; for instance, Grasmere, in the heart of the Lake District, recently suffered an outbreak and its red squirrel population is thought to now amount to just twelve individuals. But stories like Anglesey are heartening, and all thanks to the hard work of people like Holly. Whilst the debate on whether we should control one species in order to save another rages on, research is going into how we might be able to naturally protect the population. The case of pine martens, for example, is a relatively new strategy undergoing testing. The pine marten is a carnivorous mammal, belonging to the same family as mink, otters and badgers, and is making a comeback to Britain following decades of habitat loss and predator control, which devastated its population. Where it was reintroduced to Ireland, it's strongly believed that it has had a powerful impact on the grey squirrel population. Pine martens seem to prefer a dinner of grey over red squirrel, possibly because the former is a little slower and cumbersome thanks to its larger size, and therefore easier to catch. The pine marten, therefore, could be a potential solution to our grey squirrel problem, although whether this eager predator would be accepted by all of Britain remains to be seen...

Either way, it would be amazing to see more of our native species inhabiting our woodland. Red squirrels are an important part of our natural heritage, and such a lovely animal to see – I, for one, would love my nieces and nephews to enjoy them as part of the wild, not just scampering across the pages of a story book.

Red Squirrels where and when

Where…Squirrels like secluded spots of forest and woodland, off the beaten track and away from human activity. Find yourself a quiet spot away from dog-walkers and cyclists. Look out for 'pinch-points' – linear features such as the places where branches overarching the path meet, or the spaces on trunks where branches begin, that squirrels utilise to get about. There are also many places that have specific feeders for red squirrels, and are ideal spots to catch sight of them. Some great places are:

* **Cluny House gardens, Aberfeldy:** I've been here myself and can vouch for the ease of spotting red squirrels. The owners are extremely lovely and will show you round their gardens, which has been carefully managed to maintain alpine plants. Squirrels, robins and brown hares love these gardens, and are quite familiar with its owners so come closer than those in other places.

* **Aira Force, Lake District:** make use of their wildlife hide, which looks right out onto the feeders and has its own squirrel ranger.

* **Loch of the Lowes, Dunkeld:** this reserve has its own feeding boxes and rope walkways for the squirrels, which you can watch from the warmth of the woodland feeding station with its massive viewing window.

* **Formby, Liverpool:** Red squirrels are known to come out here in early morning, high in the trees.

* **Borthwood Copse, Isle of Wight:** like Anglesey, the island is free of greys and the forests carefully managed to ensure reds thrive. Hazel trees are 'coppiced' to guarantee a good crop for them to nibble.

When…Red squirrels can be seen all year round, but the best time is autumn – the leaves are sparse making them easier to spot, and they are generally active and too busy to notice observers. To a lesser extent, late winter is also when they are preoccupied, this time courting one another. Pick a clear, bright day, as they are less active during cold, wet weather, and head out during the morning when they are most active. Mostly, remember squirrels are incredibly shy and hate disturbance. Leave noisy companions, like dogs, at home and crouch quietly – they may take a little while to come out.

Things that go bump in the night

The natural world has always held an endless fascination for me, not least because there is so much to learn about, so much to see, and there is always something going on. The activity doesn't stop at sundown, when 'diurnal' animals like you and me retire to bed – far from it, in fact. As we cosy up for the night, resting our weary bodies, a whole other collection of creatures is waking, stretching themselves and gearing up for a long night's work. These are the nocturnal beasties, the ones who sleep peacefully through daylight hours and head out to do their business under the cloak of darkness. And these animals have always held a special lustre. There is something about that word – nocturnal – that speaks of secrets untold, of mysterious goings-on and furtive characters that lurk in the shadows. The idea that there is a whole world that operates surreptitiously under our noses as we sleep is irresistible to me, and I will jump at the chance to explore it for myself.

One animal that symbolises this ideology better than any other is the bat. Perhaps due to the connotations that go along with being nocturnal, it is synonymous with Hallowe'en and spooky fictions – the most obvious of course being the vampire – and people generally find them a bit creepy, or even fearsome. Vampire bats do exist; feeding on the blood of other animals like cattle and goats and, very, very rarely, humans. But they consist of only three species (the common, white-winged and the gloriously named hairy-legged vampire bat) and are restricted to the Americas, in places like Mexico, Chile and Argentina. And when you consider that there are roughly 1,300 species of bat in the whole world (and they're the ones we know about), having a mere three that actually suck blood seems a lot less worrisome. The rest of the bat world are mostly insectivores, feasting on insects, or frugivores (fruit-eaters). And as a result, they play some really vital ecological roles – controlling the numbers of insect pests, like mosquitos and midges, and acting as pollinators and seed dispersers for flowering plants. In fact, many tropical plants depend solely on bats for the survival of their race.

A lot of people don't realise that we have these ecological champions so close to home, or at least so many of them. We have no less than seventeen species of bat which breed here in the UK, all insect-eaters but all with their own unique niches, calls, flight patterns, and appearances. Yet many of us – apart from a devoted subset of the population – don't know that much about them, and a fair amount find them a bit shiver-inducing and unsavoury. Over coffee once, I asked one of my oldest and best friends why this was. She has a deep mistrust of all things non-human, and absolutely hates the outdoors (people often ask why we're friends; obviously, there's some truth to the old saying 'opposites attract'). She is my oracle on the perceptions of the 'other half'. On the subject of bats, she wrinkled up her nose in disgust and said, "Well, they're just a bit weird, aren't they? A bit sinister...I mean, nothing that furry should fly. That's a fact."

I steadied myself, took a big gulp of coffee, and asked, "Why not?"

She pondered this carefully before answering. "Well, they're like a

great big ruddy moth, aren't they? There's something not right about them, just like there's something not right about moths. Except these can bite you right? They can give you rabies? They're like a moth on steroids then. A big, dangerous moth."

Not for the first time in our friendship, I was stunned by this logic in many ways. Firstly, by the fear that bats will bite you. As I mentioned earlier, it is extremely rare to be bitten by a bat – unless you are holding one, in which case I think the bat has a right to be a little affronted. Secondly, by the idea that bats can give you rabies. Truthfully, there is a slight possibility – but it is so miniscule that it barely is worth the effort of worrying about. All our bats are intensely monitored, and there are all sorts of regulations in place for if there was ever a rabies outbreak. Also, only a teeny number of bats have ever been found to carry a particular strain of the rabies virus (I'm talking less than twenty, for the whole country) and the only way for it to be passed on is through bites or scratches. As bats are incredibly non-aggressive and wouldn't touch humans with a barge-pole – even if you occupy the same house – the only chance you have of getting it is if you're regularly handling them, which unless you're a licensed professional you really shouldn't be (if you're reading this whilst cuddling a bat, please put it down).

Lastly, I was astounded by the idea that bats are horrible to look at. Maybe my brain is wired a different way, but I've always thought they err on the right side of 'ugly'. Yes, they might be a bullet-shaped ball of fuzz with wrinkled, leathery skin attached to make wings, and a face that looks like it's been bashed in from too many encounters with a brick wall – but I think they're amazingly cute with it. Some are even decorated with hideously weird facial ornaments. Take the horseshoe bat, whose name comes from the horse-shoe shaped 'nose leaf' (a structure that is thought to help focus sound) that gives its face the unfortunate impression of having caved in on itself. But look at an image of them close-up, and I think they have the endearing look of an American football player – broad and flat of face, with a slightly dopey look that comes from being hit in the face with a hard ball one too many times. This portrayal is slightly belied by the call they make, which when heard through a bat detector sounds like a shrill witch's cackle.

Some bats could even be called conventionally cute, especially when roosting. I remember caving in South Africa, the beam of my head torch illuminating the ceiling with its groupings of hanging bats, dangling upside-down like clusters of cotton balls. Bats are very social animals, huddling together in roosts for warmth and spending many hours grooming themselves. It's a common misconception that bats are dirty; they are actually fastidiously clean. Plus, our species are all relatively small. Even are 'largest' species, the noctule, would still only fit in the palm of your hand, and our smallest – the common pipistrelle – is no bigger than a 20p piece, weighing just 5 grams. With their wee faces and snub noses, large round ears and tiny clawed feet, I actually find them downright adorable.

One of the other selling points about bats is that they are, as far as wildlife goes, quite easy to see. They make up a huge portion of our resident mammal population – 20 per cent of the entire world's mammalian life is bats – and they choose to roost in a whole variety of habitats, from echoing caves to damp tunnels, hollow trees to barns and buildings. Bats love crevices of any kind, and like to roost in the attics of old houses, behind the eaves, or the gaps between the roof tiles. The wall cavities of dilapidated farmhouses and crumbling outbuildings are also inviting, and churches – with their high ceilings and cavernous roof spaces – are almost perfect, which is why you can see so many flitting about graveyards. This probably doesn't help their spooky reputation, however.

They may be associated with Hallowe'en, but it would you'd be less likely to see a bat out at that time of year – they are most active during spring and summer. Come the colder months, following mating season in the autumn, bats will begin to slow down in preparation for winter hibernation. What happens is really quite amazing. They slow their metabolism right down, just to the bare minimum needed to survive and existing solely on their fat reserves – a bit like a car left in neutral with the engine running. This cold, sluggish state of being is known as 'torpid' and to get there successfully, the bats have to feast themselves silly in the months they are active. The best time to see them is in late spring, soon after they've come out of hibernation and need to re-stock their fat reserves. After months of sleep, they're ravenous and are super active, catching up to 3,000 insects a night; gorging themselves on flies, moths and even spiders.

This habit of roosting in human dwellings means that it's the job of some to investigate, monitor and protect these sites; making sure old, decrepit buildings aren't knocked down if they contain a bat roost, or helping people to live alongside the ones installed in the loft. This also gives us a great opportunity to further understand these fascinating creatures, learning more about our native species and contributing to national surveys. I am fortunate enough to call some of these ecological consultants and bat monitors close friends, and in the past I've been lucky to have been invited out on surveys. I've always found them a very interesting, if not unusual, way to spend an evening.

I must admit, I knew next to nothing about these little winged creatures. My experience came to some power point slides in a single lecture and a rather sad-looking, withered specimen, who we unfortunately butchered for a lab dissection (don't worry, he was already dead). Thus, my knowledge extended to a few hastily scribbled bullet-points and the strong smell of formaldehyde. So it was with an empty head that I embarked on my first-ever bat survey on a warm, summer's evening in June.

Our site was a disintegrating, derelict farmhouse, with windows clouded by dust and grime and knee-deep in rough pasture. I was shown briefly by my friend's rather eccentric boss how to shine my torch up onto the roof tiles to search for the tiny gap where a bat may have squeezed through, or any holes in the eaves. We conducted a thorough search of the inside of the building too, which smelled like daylight had been trapped in there for years and still contained a dirty oil-lamp, half buried in wood-shavings, on the rough-hewn table. We were looking for tell-tale signs of bat roosts. These are mainly droppings, which are usually black and crumbly, different from rodent droppings which will 'smear' when you touch them (as I said, an unusual way to spend an evening). Another sign is a pile of insect wing cases on the floor, which are usually found underneath a bats' 'feeding perch' where they will sit to enjoy their dinner, particularly larger prey. I could just imagine a bat tucking into a good meal, tearing into the softer body and discarding the tougher bits, spitting them over the side like a medieval king would discard meat bones.

Then, as light faded, I was given a crash-course in how to use a bat detector, and left at my station watching the entrance to the building. I was left with nothing but a fold-up camping chair and a worryingly inquisitive bull in the field behind me, who would snort at intervals and make me jump and contemplate the strength of the rickety fence between us. Luckily, I was rescued by my friend, who left his post at the other corner of the building to come and sit with me, and educate me on the wonder of bats. As the sky changed from dusky pink to inky blue, we tuned our bat detectors into the right frequencies and waited for the show to start, listening to the white noise hiss and crackle, and the far-off shout of a pheasant.

Bat detectors are undeniably cool. They are essentially a piece of technology that allows you to tune into an animal language normally undetectable by human hearing. Bats use sonar to communicate, navigate and catch their prey. Hunting in the dark, they are essentially blind, but by firing out ultrasonic sound-waves they can tell the location, distance and even the direction in which the desired item is going – all from how the sound is reflected off the object and returns to the bat's ears. It's like throwing a ball off a wall with your eyes closed; the closer you stand, the faster the ball will bounce off and come back to you. The further away, the longer the rebound. Echolocation (to give it its fancy name) has the same principle, but the accuracy with which they do this is astonishing – catching flies on the wing without even being able to see them. But the vocalisations used are so high-pitched only dogs and, occasionally, young children can hear them. Using a detector, you feel like you're in MI5 listening into a hidden microphone, hearing things you shouldn't.

The best time to see bats is generally around twenty minutes after sunset; it's still light enough to see silhouettes against the twilight sky, and the right time to see an outpouring of bats as they escape their daytime roosts. Sure enough, as the farmhouse became a deep shadow, a flurry of small shapes began to fire out of the side of the building as rapid as machine gun bullets, and began to dart erratically about the surrounding air space. Simultaneously, our bat detectors erupted with clicks, the volume ebbing and flowing as the maker wheeled overhead. Different species will call with different frequencies, which enables the researcher to identify them. Here, we'd anticipated two separate species – the common pipistrelle, and the long-eared brown bat. The former – as the name suggests – is the most common species of bat to the UK, incorporating up to 75 per cent of sightings. They are also our smallest, with a minute wingspan of just 7-10 inches, and fly at high speeds with jerky, darting movements as they pursue small flies, like midges (which makes them a hero if you live in Scotland). They'll frequently catch prey on the wing in a behaviour called 'aerial hawking' – not unlike swallows – and are found in areas where these insects congregate, along treelines and hedgerows or above water. That night, I was in charge of the pipistrelles, my detector tuned into their 'golden range' of 45kHz. It seemed like they were having a field day, enjoying the bounty that must have been delivered by the enormous, shaggy hedgerow bordering the farmhouse (untamed, it seemed, for many years). My detector was exploding with their calls, which sound like a series of clicks ending in lower, wetter slapping sounds, like a flag whipping against a pole in strong wind. Eventually as the light disappeared completely we were left with just the popping noises to tell us they were still present. Just like them, we were pretty much blind, relying on sound. Much later I looked up a picture, to put a face to the call. To me they looked like teddy-bears; pale, reddish-brown with a round face and broad, flat muzzle, and miniscule, pin-hole eyes; I guess they're not much needed when you spend most of your time in the dark.

My new colleague and teacher of all things bat oversaw a different species. The brown long-eared bat, who also frequents old buildings and barns, is much larger than the pint-sized pipistrelle with a wingspan of 9-11 inches, and, naturally, has a lower voice. My partner had his detector tuned into 30kHz, and in times when mine was quiet I could hear the characteristic rapid burst of clicks, something like the sound a Geiger counter makes. He told me that this species was distinctly lazier than some others, sometimes using just the sound emitted by the insect's wings to detect them, or even landing on the ground and waiting for some foolish soul to come to them. Their broader wings enable them to have slower flight with greater manoeuvrability, allowing them to hover amongst bushes and pluck insects from the leaves and stems. They eat a great variety of things; moths, beetles, earwigs, even spiders. Straining my eyes in what light was left, I could just about see their bigger silhouettes gliding lower, skimming the hedgerow to glean the insects from it. Without much light, however, it was near impossible to see the enormous pointed ears they are famous for. They are almost the entire length of their body, giant appendages that dwarf the bat's face making it look almost comically tiny in comparison, like an African bat-eared fox in miniature (I guess, in hindsight, this is where that fox gets its name). These, he informed me, are particularly fond of loft spaces – he'd visited the house of an old lady a few weeks previously, who was most aggrieved at having a colony of around twenty little faces peering back at her.

It's important we ensure these roosts persevere, as they are so important to bat ecology. Not only do they serve as places in which to hibernate, but they also function as nurseries. In the early summer months females will create maternity roosts in which to raise their young, who are fed on their mother's milk until they are strong enough to fly themselves (which in some species is the ripe old age of three weeks old!). The males, however, stay well away, instead forming bachelor pads elsewhere – well, except for brown long-ears, who seem to have a slightly more modern society.

With all these important functions, it's no wonder that some of our bat populations are threatened following changes to them. Pipistrelles, for example, are declining because of their reliance on buildings, which makes them vulnerable to renovation and toxic chemicals used in processes like the treatment of wooden rafters. Both they and brown long-eared bats are also susceptible to the modernisation of agriculture, which has destroyed available roosting and feeding habitat. However, there is one species of bat that seems to be benefitting from industrialisation – the Daubenton's, or 'water bat'. Summer colonies can be found roosting near bodies of water – in tunnels, caves, mines and cellars – where they snatch aquatic insects hovering above the water, or even scoop them from it using their tail or feet. Man-made quarries and reservoirs have provided artificial roosting sites, benefitting this species somewhat.

There is so much more to learn about bats, so many species – I could write a whole book about just them. They are incredible creatures. Amazingly skilled hunters with all manner of weird and wonderful adaptions (I urge you to look up 'nose-leaves' on google), yet sociable souls who live in tight-knit groups. Not to mention, they are a vitally important part of our ecosystem. Just don't let their reputation fool you...

I would like to end this chapter by talking about an animal that is the antithesis of the bat; a nocturnal animal that is liked by almost everyone, but should come with a more fearsome repute. I have had two chances to see this animal in the wild. The first was sitting in that camping chair by the farmhouse waiting for bats. It was right at the start of the evening, while the sun was still bleeding into the horizon and the sky tinged with its red-orange glow. It surprised us – a great, white shape tore out of the adjacent barn and flew directly overhead, travelling at great speed but making no sound, like a ghost. We nearly fell out of our chairs, my friend dropping his flask with a loud clang. It didn't return, but later we explored the barn from which it had came, shining our torches into the rafters. And in there, we heard bursts of a sharp, rasping sound, not unlike steam escaping from a kettle, emanating from atop a thick plank of wood that ran across the ceiling. Our suspicions were further confirmed by a collection of downy feathers that had drifted down onto the straw beneath, and a smattering of slimy, white-grey droppings. We were standing below a barn owl nest.

Whilst I never saw that particular barn owl again, I did get a second opportunity to catch sight of one in the wild. My friend Dan – who works as an ecologist down in Worcester – has a deep passion for owls of all shapes and sizes, and had promised me a sighting when I last visited. Dan is incredibly knowledgeable about birds, and is one of those people who will casually identify bird calls with the ease of a commentator in a football match. If there was anyone I'd trust to find me an owl, it'd be him. We set off again about an hour before sunset, that golden hour when the light filters gently through the trees, everything seems to slow down as a haze settles over the landscape. Our destination was a large stretch of open, tussocky grassland – prime owl hunting country. Barn owls usually predate on small rodents, including field voles, mice and shrews, who hang about in such habitat. We set up camp by an oak tree on top of a small hill, which gave us panoramic views of the area, and waited.

I queried as to how Dan could be so sure we'd see an owl that night.

Barn Owl.

Female barn owl hunting.

To my untrained eye, it looked devoid of any activity at all; it was a mellow summer's evening, and in the absence of any breeze the grass remained distinctly unruffled, hardly teeming with voles. Dan simply grinned and let me in on his fool-proof method. "If I see kestrels hunting in the area, I know there's probably a good chance of seeing barn owls ... they share the same niche. And I saw some this afternoon." And, as it turns out, his method is 'fool-proof' for a reason...

We heard the owl before we saw it. Now, I've heard barn owls described as 'angelic' and 'ethereal', but their call is anything but. Unlike other owls, it does not hoot but screeches; a high-pitched, grating sound, like fingernails on a black board. But the sight of one? Now that's something. Some twenty minutes later, she appeared, gliding on silent wings, just close enough to be mesmerised by her beautiful features. A pale golden back, flecked with silvery grey and black; a luminous white, heart-shaped face with two round black eyes, like buttons on a snowman. It can be difficult to tell the difference between male and female, but Dan – wielding a pair of binoculars – deduced it was probably a 'she' on account of the speckles on her chest. Those of the males are almost completely snow-white.

We watched as she soared across the field, scanning the grass intently for animals our lesser eyes couldn't see. Barn owls are beautiful, but deadly; silent killers extremely well-equipped for the job. A low wing loading – which means very large wings for a very light body – allows them to fly slowly and hover effortlessly with just the slightest bit of lift from the air, so they can spot prey effectively. Their body feathers are tremendously soft and adapted to deaden the sound of rushing air, not only to sneak up on unwitting prey but also to hear their movements far below on the ground, unhindered. For this same purpose, barn owls have specialised hearing systems – the most sensitive of any animal ever recorded, actually. Firstly, that heart-shaped face acts as a big satellite dish, the stiff, short feathers collecting sound and directing it to the ears. Secondly, the ears themselves are positioned so that one is just above the other and sound reaches them in different ways, allowing the owl to hone in on the exact location of the unsuspecting animal beneath.

As we watched, she focussed in on something, hovering above the ground with her wings twitching imperceptibly in the thermals of the air. Target secured, she divebombed steeply into the grass, feet first, and emerged seconds later with something small and struggling grasped in her powerful talons. Then, she was off, gliding elegantly into the last of the fading sun. I turned and beamed at Dan; I knew he'd be able to get me a sighting, but not one this good. Definitely deserving of the beer I bought him in the pub afterwards!

Spotting bats and owls

Seeing both bats and owls requires patience, a willingness to forego sleep, and a flask of something hot…

✳ For bats, the best time of year is late spring to early summer, when they have just come out of hibernation and are feasting to restore fat reserves. They are very active during this time. Try at dusk, around 20 minutes after sunset, when the light is just enough to see silhouettes. Anywhere where insects gather – field boundaries, hedgerows, bodies of water – are your best bet.

✳ Barn owls require a little more luck. You're most likely to see them hunting in open country; pastureland, along riverbank edges (where the voles will be hiding) and sometimes roadside verges. Get a good vantage point with broad views of the whole area. The 'golden hour' is about an hour before sunset. You can generally see barn owls throughout the year, right up until November, and they are one of the more widely distributed owl species – your chances could be good!

How to help them

There are multiple ways to help bats! Think of things that will encourage their food source: insects. Plant flowers that are fragrant at night, let your garden get a bit unruly in patches, or even build a pond. Try to reduce your use of chemical pesticides, too. And build a bat box – there are many different types available commercially and to DIY. Check out the **Bat Conservation Trust** for tips and advice.

For barn owls, look to the rodent population. If possible, allow grass to grow to encourage mice and voles and ensure that, if you are using pest control, that it is non-toxic. You can also erect a nesting box, at least 4m off the ground and ideally beside rough grassland. There are ones to buy online, or the **Barn Owl Trust** have free plans on their website.

URBAN SPACES

This is the chapter I was most excited to write. The whole purpose of this book is to show that you don't need a great deal of time or fancy equipment to enjoy and appreciate nature – it's there, all around us, we only need to open our eyes.

The word 'wildlife', I think, can be confusing. It conjures up images of the deep, dark tangle of a jungle or the vast open plains of the savannah, where great predators prowl, odd-looking primates swing between the trees and everything is huge, vibrantly coloured and probably poisonous. I've been fortunate to experience some of these wild places for myself. Delving into the close, humid greenery of the forests in Madagascar, I've stepped over vivid chameleons and ducked under spiders larger than my fist. I've bounced around in the back of a prehistoric range rover on safari, where every twist and turn revealed yet another exciting encounter – a white rhino with offspring in tow, or a pride of lions devouring an elephant carcass. These are the images that 'wildlife' usually brings to mind, the ones that we're most likely to see in a David Attenborough documentary. Even back on home ground, wildlife is something we see as confined to our nature reserves and the places people don't go. We see it as something that needs to be sought out; discovered only when clad in hiking boots and an anorak, or admired via an Instagram feed.

But our natural world is changing. Our cities and urban dwellings have spread, oozing over their boundaries and encroaching onto wild spaces like an oil spill. New housing developments, roads, shopping complexes … the list of construction is endless. But it's a two-way street. Nature has had to make do with this change, and we share our cities and towns with more species than you realise. 'Wildlife' is here too, just waiting to be noticed. You don't even have to leave the house to see it.

Our gardens are jungles – albeit on a slightly smaller scale – filled with all manner of minibeasts fluttering and buzzing and squirming. Peer under a rock or a leaf and you could watch the busy comings and goings of insect life, from the awe-inspiring weight lifting skills of ants to the curious snaking movements of millipedes. Garden birds of all shapes and sizes can be chronicled throughout the year, performing dainty courtship rituals or battling with one another over territory. And one of the silver linings to climate change and other human-induced issues is that we are seeing more weird and wonderful birds visit our gardens, from all over the world. Furthermore, it seems like some of these exotic guests are here to stay – demonstrated by the green parakeets that frequent several parts of London.

Don't have a garden? Well, birds are literally everywhere. They nest in chimneys, under bridges ... and sometimes great flocks erupt from these places at dusk, with species such as starlings taking to the skies in unfathomable numbers. Peregrine falcons are stalking the skies of our busiest metropolises, feasting on the rich pickings offered by other more portly, cooing residents. And nature has its own night-life, too. Bushy-tailed urban scavengers skulk in the shadows and take advantage of the over-flowing bins; bats carve patterns above the skyline; and hedgehogs snuffle their way along our pavements, little bumbling bundles of spines and inquisitive noses.

And where humans have vacated spaces, nature has reclaimed it. Find any abandoned construction site or building, and guaranteed, plants will be sprouting. Leggy ox-eye daisies and dandelions push their way up through the rubble; buddleia pokes out of extinct chimney tops. Nature recolonises quickly, and what started as a wasteland can become an overgrown oasis in a matter of months. A new nature.

So, whilst we can marvel at the wild things that hang about the highlands, reside by our rivers or cosy up in our forests, we must also admire and appreciate our urban companions. But although some have thrived in this brick-and-cement environment, others are suffering. House sparrows, for example, used to be a regular feature of our hedges, chattering away noisily. Now they are quieted, and have shown one of the fastest declines of any common garden bird. It's no secret either that butterflies and bees are fast disappearing, and that impacts a whole host of other insects and birds, too. And our favourite wee spikey pal, the hedgehog? Sadly, a rare sight nowadays. It's not just our wild habitats that need help, but our urban ones too – we need to be thinking more about how we can incorporate wildlife into our plans, and make it a safe haven for them, too. And it all starts by getting to know our neighbours.

City slickers

My third year of Uni got off to an unfortunate start, when I was jerked awake by a blood-curdling screech coming through my bedroom window at the ungodly hour of 3am. Being rudely awakened by such a terrible sound isn't an enjoyable experience for anybody, but for me it was compounded by the fact that I was home alone – my flatmate was at her boyfriend's house that night.

We'd also just moved into a new place, which gave a whole new meaning to 'student digs' with its threadbare carpets, mismatched furniture, and distinct musty smell that never went away no matter how many candles we lit. To access the flat, you had to ascend a decrepit staircase that creaked and groaned in protest at every step, the plaster cracking ominously in places. And if the couple upstairs walked too heavily great clouds of dust would fall from our ceiling like miniature snowstorms. It was not in the best area, either; as students, we'd gone for cheap and cheerful as opposed to 'nice neighbourhood, good schools'. The street name – Sunnyside Road – was deceivingly family friendly. Police cars were familiar fixtures, and underage neds (or chavs, to anyone South of the border) would congregate outside the corner shop we lived above, forever on a misguided quest to obtain alcohol. So, when I awoke to a chilling scream emanating from our back garden, I threw myself out of bed and made a rapid assessment of all the escape routes and potential 'weapons' in my room. Clutching a bedside lamp with my heart pounding in my ears, I made my way over to the open bedroom window and peered cautiously round the curtains.

My room looked down onto our garden, which we had fondly nicknamed 'Sunnyside jungle'. It was a gloriously overgrown tangle of leggy dandelions and rosebay willow-herb vying for the sunlight, and weeds pushing their way aggressively through some abandoned furniture that had been carelessly discarded. Dense clusters of nettles and thick, spiky thistles exploded out of a rotten sofa that sagged morosely under the weight of rainstorms past, and oxford ragwort had buried a broken television set that looked like it had last been used in the early 90s. Under the artificial glow of the streetlight, it looked quite intimidating, as if it was hiding a multitude of menaces between the jumble of stalks and leaves. And yet, as I stood there and peered into its murky depths, there was not even the faintest whisper of movement. My blood pressure came down, my heart slowed, and

I lowered the lamp ... but then, almost on cue, I heard it again; that high-pitched chilling wail, the sort that made the hairs on the back of my neck stand on end and goose bumps erupt all over my arms. This, however, was not a sound made by humans, but the call of a fox. A female fox, to be exact.

It's no wonder that many folk – myself included – are fooled by this noise. In the dead of night, it is an eerie, bone-chilling shriek that echoes around neighbourhoods and street corners, sounding exactly like a damsel in distress. Even when identified as a fox call, the sound can be misleading. It was once a common misconception that it was made by the female during sex in reaction to the male's barbed penis. This does indeed sound like a torture device, and is present in many other species (lions are another example). It is basically a horrible form of insurance policy for the male, ensuring that even if his chosen partner has second thoughts, she can't get away and his genes will still be passed on (sex to much of the animal kingdom is a crude and unromantic affair, it has to be said). Many thought that the vixen's cry was an expression of pain and discomfort, when it is quite the opposite. It is actually her way of signalling to all the males in the area that she is in season, or 'available' – essentially, the fox equivalent of flirting. Quite why it is such a spooky, toe-curling noise is beyond me ... but then again, so much of the animal world is baffling to us mere humans.

The owner of this cry appeared moments later, slinking out of the thick vegetation and stepping daintily over our garden gate, which had come off its hinges months ago, and lay on the ground rotting, splintered and totally ineffective, doing nothing to soothe my nerves. I watched her trot down the street, her auburn fur flaring periodically as she passed under the streetlights, evidently off to meet a potential suitor. Suddenly I felt exhausted; my protective lamp discarded, I collapsed back into bed, trying not to think of the fact that I had to be up again in three hours. The following morning, I stumbled into my lecture, a little bleary eyed, to find that – ironically – it was about foxes.

Urban foxes are one of those species that people either love unconditionally, or loathe with a passion – they are the Marmite of the natural world. Unsurprisingly, I belong to the former tribe. Urban foxes, to me, signify something very special; a secret wilderness within the city, a reminder that nature is never very far away. They are beautiful, ethereal creatures, their fur a shimmering copper-auburn as though kissed by fire, their almond-shaped eyes a bright amber. No bigger than a large cat, they are slight, delicate creatures with a slender muzzle and small paws on which they pad silently about the

street, or balance tenderly on walls and rooftops. And of course, they are famous for that bushy feather-duster of a tail, the end of which is dipped in black.

I always love to see a fox. Perhaps it's the elusive nature of them; seeing one is relatively rare, as they are most active at dawn and dusk, those otherworldly times of day when the rest of the city sleeps and the streets are so quiet you could almost hear a pin drop. I often used to see one on my way home from the pub in the early hours, tiptoeing about the shadows searching for scraps (the fox, not me, although I was partial to our local takeaway after a few pints). Seeing one at this time of the night – or morning, to be precise – was something magical. The streets emptied, no cars on the road ... just me and the fox and the quiet stillness of the night. It felt like a secret almost, a fleeting glimpse into the clandestine world of wildlife in the city. That being said, they are the one of the most abundant mammalian carnivores in the world, with dense populations sharing some of our biggest cities with us. It is estimated that there are 10,000 in London alone – that's 16 per square mile. They thrive mainly because they are distinctly un-fussy eaters, eating a huge variety of food from rats and pigeons to dogfood and table scraps. Barely anything is off-menu, which means they can colonise almost anywhere and still get by. A common perception of the fox is that it is a dirty bin-dweller, ransacking rubbish bags and strewing the remnants across the street. But this is so often not the case – if you want the true culprit, look to gulls. Foxes should instead be admired for their resourcefulness. They've been known to uproot earthworms from the ground in spring, snack on beetles, and even nip blackberries from roadside bushes in autumn. Think of them as natural pest control, too, as they are partial to the 'disease-ridden' pests many of us have come to fear – imagine London's rat problem if they weren't around!

Admittedly, foxes do have a less savoury habit regarding food. I used to have a cousin that lived in Bristol, which is home to the BBC's Natural History Unit for a reason – it's chock full of wildlife. I was excited to visit him and experience it for myself, and I was not disappointed. He lived in the leafy green haven of suburbia, with its plethora of garden birds and stalking peregrine falcons, and a resident badger that nearly dented the car on our drive back from the train station. But my cousin had a hidden agenda behind my invitation. For months, he informed me, his garden had been plagued by a mysterious criminal, who dug holes all over it with vigour and filled them with rotting corpses. I was promptly shown the evidence after dinner – a disaster scene of torn up earth and various, maggot-infested 'bodies', most of which looked like rats or voles, but one that looked suspiciously like the carcass of a roast chicken complete with a lone segment of parsnip. I had an inkling as to the culprit, and suggested we leave out a small dish of food and wait until night fell.

As the light faded and the black cloak of night began to envelop the garden, we perched on the patio steps, cradling cups of coffee, and waited, staring at a chicken leg we'd left in the middle of the lawn. My cousin was under strict instructions to remain quiet (my nan used to say he could talk the hind legs off a donkey) and I could practically hear him struggling to supress whatever comments popped into his mind, instead slurping on his drink louder than I would have liked. But despite this, out the shady perpetrator came – a dog fox, creeping cautiously out the shadows, his amber eyes twinkling in the light from the house. Foxes, to me, always look like they're up to something; eyes narrowed as if conjuring up a cunning plan, ears pricked upright as though in fear of getting caught. This one tiptoed across the grass, picking his way across so slowly and carefully he reminded me of a burglar out to steal the crown jewels, every step potentially a crucial mistake. I spotted him earlier than my cousin, who seemed more concerned with a hang-nail on his thumb, but when he did eventually look up I pre-empted the inevitably loud and audible gasp he was about

to make, pinching him on the arm to stop him. This did not have the desired effect – instead, he yelped out in pain.

Our visitor stopped stock-still, fur bristling, and registered our presence. For a few moments we just looked at one another – luckily my cousin had the sense to stay silent – the fox with his front paw dangling in mid-air, soot-black nose twitching imperceptibly as he tried to tell if we were friend or foe. Apparently though, the smell of the chicken was too overpowering to bear. Deciding to take the risk he stretched forwards, deftly taking the offering with sharp canines, and then turned tail and vanished back into the shadows, the meal safely clamped in his jaws. The following morning, we discovered the very same leg half-heartedly buried in the petunias, to which, oddly, my cousin took offence. I assured him that his chicken was very tasty – the very fact the fox buried it made it so. Foxes will 'cache' their food; burying morsels to save for later, especially if they have a surplus. And they aren't that bothered about sell-by dates, hence the rotten offerings that had been scattered about his garden.

After this, my cousin rather took to the fox, and in the month that followed, I received weekly updates on his antics. Some were more welcome than others – he had a habit of sending details of the decaying messes left behind, just as I was about to start my own dinner.

During stints working at BBC Scotland, I was often out and about at 'fox hours', and I became quite accustomed to them. Glasgow – where the main office building is situated – is a hotspot for vulpine life, with its ideal recipe of large green spaces such as Kelvingrove park, and a vast array of food on offer.

In my position as researcher, I often had lengthy days away on shoots, which meant waking up before the sun came out and returning home long after it had gone to bed. Early morning was the hour of the dog foxes, patrolling their territories before the hurried stream of commuters filled the streets. Foxes do not hunt in packs, preferring to go it alone. But they keep territories in family groups: often a mother, father, cubs, and a few non-breeding vixens. The family keeps in touch through sound and scent, calling to one another and using urine to ward intruders off and let them know 'these grounds are taken'. Adult males will keep their territories by stalking the perimeter, and I would see them padding about on my way to work, peeking surreptitiously around street corners or sniffing at bins. The best 'pads' were clearly ones that contained the enormous, industrial kind – so often brimming over with all manner of tasty offerings – and I even saw a few fights surrounding them when a rogue male tried his chances. Whilst young vixens may remain in the home territory, sub adult males will often fly the nest and roam further afield in search of a home of their own, which sometimes brings them into conflict with the established elders.

I couldn't help but feel sorry for these youngsters. They begin life in quite a cushioned environment, enclosed in a cosy den below the earth. In the countryside, you may find these nestled amongst tree roots or beneath bushes; in the city, dens are made in railway embankments or, more commonly, underneath garden sheds. Being a freelancer, I was only in Glasgow for a few weeks at a time, meaning I crashed on the sofas of very kind friends. One such friend lived in the West end, which seemed to have a higher concentration of foxes than anywhere else. One time in the early spring, we suspected there was a fox den beneath the dilapidated old shed at the bottom of the rectangular garden she shared with the other residents of her block of flats. Late at night, a female would dash in and out from what appeared to be an entrance, masked from prying eyes by a thick bed of nettles. She would rush into the garden with something in her mouth – presumably something nourishing for her offspring – and vanish underneath, pausing briefly at the entrance to glance left and right and check she hadn't been discovered. Not wanting to disturb her or stress out the cubs, we left the den well alone, no matter how much I was dying to see inside.

In late spring, once they have grown in size and strength, the cubs will venture out from the den and explore their immediate surroundings. Playfighting is one of the best ways to prepare them for the challenges of later life, including those territorial stand-offs around the bins. They will rough and tumble, nipping at one another's ears and neck in an undeniably cute display. And at this stage, they are fed and watered dutifully by their mother, allowing them to time to mature and grow in confidence in blissful security. But come autumn, once they've reached maturity, Mum and Dad seem to decide they've grown too big for their boots and they're turfed out. Sometimes, the parents will even become aggressive in an effort to chase them away. This seems to turn the young fox into quite the anguished teenager, forming gangs and causing trouble, biting through things and devouring easy pickings from bins and forgotten takeaway cartons.

At night, Glasgow is a different city; the businessmen and hazy quiet of the morning replaced by neon lights, the greasy smell of fried food and periodic bursts of warm air and loud conversation as the doors of pubs are opened and shut. The streets are thick with people and taxis, the heavy buzz of traffic and workdays escaped.

The foxes seemed different too. In the early hours, with nothing but the bin-men and the occasional, sleepy-eyed researcher to disturb them, they appeared confident, a little bolder. But at night they seemed more secretive, sticking to the shadows and remaining wary of the crowds that spilled noisily from the bars. The name given to a collection of foxes is a 'basic skulk', and this never seemed more appropriate than in the depths of night, watching them lurk as close as they dared in the hopes of securing some scraps to eat. One of the reasons this species might have thrived in such urban dwellings is because people feed them – whether that be a chip thrown casually, or a plate of dog food deliberately left out on the back step. As I said, foxes aren't picky eaters; they'll eat what they're given.

Returning home late from a long day's filming, shattered and famished, the prospect of cooking filled me with dread (beans on toast was a staple during those weeks). On Fridays, I'd treat myself to a takeaway from the Indian on the corner of my friend's road, whose prawn jalfrezi remains unrivalled. It was manned by an extremely friendly man, with a round, permanently beaming face and a laugh as rich as the korma sauce. I always seemed to arrive at the right time with barely any queue, in between the rush of people hungry for dinner and those needing sustenance after a night out, so we would strike up a conversation. Upon finding out I was a zoologist by trade, he proudly introduced me to 'his' fox, who he fed out the back door and fondly nicknamed 'Marmaduke'. She was perhaps one of the best fed foxes in Glasgow, as he didn't just feed her the scraps but saved small portions of meat for her – lamb shoulder, chicken cooked on the bone, tender morsels of beef. And clearly, it was beneficial; her coat shone, and she looked somewhat plumper than her scavenging counterparts. She was easily identifiable due to her one white forepaw, like a glove, and the slight nick on her right ear from a previous altercation.

Normally I would have scorned such regular feeding of a wild animal. It's a dangerous game; the animal can get far too used to humans, actively approaching them in expectation of being fed. And, unfortunately, not all people are friendly. Some mistake inquisitiveness or curiosity as aggression, placing animals in a hostile situation. But my new friend treated Marmaduke with a healthy respect, retreating back into the shop whenever she appeared and watching from the back window, and he took so much joy from watching her I hardly had the heart to get my conservationist's hat on. I was slightly mollified by the fact that she would hastily scamper off if we tried to approach her, throwing us a disgruntled look over her shoulder. For added comedic effect, her mouth would be stained from the spices in the curry like smeared lipstick – she really did give the impression of a Glaswegian night owl on her way home from a big Friday night.

Whilst feeding our wee vulpine friends might seem like a nice thing to do (and, in a humane sense, it is) they don't actually need it – there is so much food available to them that even in winter, they don't suffer. But some people hand-feed them, which sometimes can do more harm than good, encouraging them to lose that natural fear of the human race and approach closer than they maybe should. Many city councils have now asked their residents to stop feeding foxes – if anything, it brings them into further conflict with people. Foxes are frequently vilified by the media, with headlines such as 'foxes: a brush with danger' or 'fox attacks man, woman and their cat in their home' splashed across the tabloids. For every person who dotes on them, there is someone who wants them culled, and 'pest control' is the most popular result when you search for 'urban fox' on google. But fox attacks are astonishingly rare. Like any wild animal, they will attack only if they feel threatened or pushed into a corner – which is why they may go for a curious dog. And no two foxes have the same personality; whilst some may be inquisitive and even friendly, others may scare easy and not take kindly to anyone who comes too close. And the idea that our cities have become 'overrun' is unfounded. There is no substantial evidence of an increase in fox numbers, it just may seem so. We are taking over more rural areas than ever before, and the urban fox – whose only difference to those in the countryside is postcode – has naturally adapted to this change, having first colonised urban areas after the Second World War and the industrial boom that followed.

It's sad that they have such a bad reputation in our country, because they are beautiful, intelligent creatures with a fascinating life history, who have thrived on the basis of their own resourcefulness and adaptability. We should be thankful to share our streets with such admirable characters, and appreciate the magic of having a little bit of hidden wilderness within our city walls.

Finding Fantastic Mr Fox

Where…Foxes can be found in most of our major cities. London, Glasgow, Bristol, Newcastle, Edinburgh, Birmingham…the list goes on, so you should have a good chance of spotting one. Studies by Brighton and Reading universities have found Bournemouth to have the highest concentration in the UK.

✳ Check up on roofs or high walls, where they like to take a nap, or in quieter areas with bins such as the back of supermarkets. Foxes are also regular visitors to gardens; keep watching after sunset for a vulpine visitor, or look for signs such as holes dug in the soil and grey-tinged faeces (look out for small bones contained inside). You can also leave out dishes of dog food or scraps to entice them, but try not to make this a regular habit.

When…They are most active during early morning and late at night.

What to do if you find an injured fox:
Sadly, the lifespan of foxes in urban areas is only two years – those in rural areas can live up to fifteen. They are often injured by cars or even deliberately harmed: caught in snares or poisoned. If you find one, you should:

✳ Not approach. An injured animal is vulnerable, and more likely to feel threatened. Maintain a distance and if it can walk, avoid backing it into a corner

✳ Contact the RSPCA or the National Fox Welfare Society, who should be able to advise and come out to retrieve the individual. Alternatively, call your local vet.

✳ If you suspect cubs to have been abandoned or orphaned, wait and observe before alerting the authorities. The female may leave them for longer than expected.

The overgrown jungle of ivy.

The graveyard that is still very much alive...

Nature has a funny way of creeping up on you. Places that were once orderly and landscaped soon turn wild and chaotic if left to their own devices. Even the most manicured of gardens can fast become anarchy if neglected just a little. Carefully placed flowerbeds turning drunk and disorderly, growing shaggy and unkempt; rebel forces in the form of weeds pushing their way hungrily up through the ranks of choice perennials. On the surface this may appear as an overgrown mess, but it is a glorious celebration of the ability of nature to bite back where it has been oppressed, reclaiming the land bit by bit. And such places are the best places, as they can be an oasis of serendipity in an otherwise human dominated landscape, and as such, a haven for wildlife. They are often well worth exploring.

I may have lived in Scotland for over seven years now, but my roots are firmly planted in Geordie soil. I grew up in the famous seaside town of Whitley Bay, which is a fair distance outside the city and enjoys a slower pace of life as a result. As far as urban spaces go it's a pretty great one, with the eastern coastline and the North Sea on our doorstep, miles of fields and pasture surrounding it, and the Northumbrian countryside just a stone's throw away. My friends and I spent many a happy day exploring these places, coming home with grass stained knees or shoes full of sand and grinning, exalted faces.

Just down the road from my parents' house lurks one of those mysterious overgrown spots; an old graveyard. It sits under the glowering face of St Albans church and is bordered on all sides by fields full of ambling horses, and hedgerows so thick you could fill an entire freezer with blackberries come autumn, and still have some to spare. I distinctly remember early expeditions here as a little girl being extremely disappointing – rows upon rows of neat little planters, painstakingly maintained paths and trees so aggressively pruned it appeared the gardener was on a crusade for uniformity. And very little wildlife, so I took my hunt elsewhere. Running down the side of the graveyard was a rough dirt track that took you through dense hedgerows to a little babbling stream and the fields beyond, and it was more suitable to my slightly messier taste. I preferred these unruly hedges, filled to bursting with chirping, chattering birds. Sparrows (or spuggies, as we call them in the north east) spilled out from the shaggy brambles alongside coal tits, blue tits and even the occasional robin, looking oddly out of place any

The country lane at sundown.

time after Christmas. Here, the grass was long and tickled my legs. Beetles ambled lazily about the stony path, and butterflies would dance about the brambles in summertime – cabbage whites and red admirals settling on the ground to warm themselves in the sunshine, before taking off like a swirl of confetti at my arrival. If I was lucky I'd catch a fleeting glimpse of a stoat or weasel zipping across the path, or even a water vole sliding hastily down the banks of the stream. It appealed more to my wilder nature than the clipped, formal air of the graveyard (plus my dog was always bound to pee on someone's gravestone, and I was terrified there would be ghostly repercussions).

I left for University, and swapped the little country lanes with their busy hedgerows for the wilder, more dramatic landscapes of Scotland. But whenever I returned home for the holidays, I never felt truly 'home' until I'd gone for a little ramble down to my old haunt. And I noticed that slowly but surely, the graveyard had transformed from a prim and proper affair to an unruly, overgrown jungle. Down the bottom, where the newer graves had been erected, everything was still very well kept, but bordering this was a distinct line where the gardener had apparently given up the land to nature. The grass was much shaggier, made all the more obvious for the carefully clipped land right beside it. And past this, directly behind the church, lay the glorious chaos.

It begins with a trek up through that long grass. In the summer, the air is filled with dandelion seeds; evidence of thousands of shedding manes floating in the sky like an idiot's antidote to snowflakes. Wildflowers spring up in a riot of colour that seems almost inappropriate for somewhere so sombre – crimson poppies, sunshine yellow buttercups, lilac clusters of blue-bells. Butterflies and moths flit daintily about, and it was here I saw my first ever hummingbird hawk-moth. These are, without a doubt, one of the most amazing invertebrates you could ever have luck to come across. They look and act like their namesake, hovering with astonishing accuracy in front of a flower, and the darting way in which they move about a plant completes the illusion. Once a suitable meal has been selected, they set about probing their extremely lengthy, needle-thin proboscis into the flower's centre to savour the sweet nectar inside. At rest, this cumbersome mouthpiece curls up neatly into a spiral for efficient storage – a feature which, I'm sure, many hummingbirds envy, especially the sword-billed variety. They are the only bird to have a beak longer than its body, and always look slightly imbalanced. These moths favour flowers rich in nectar, and I spotted mine zipping in and out of a honeysuckle plant that had crept up the high, dry-stone wall at one side of the graveyard. Well, more accurately, I heard it first. Hummingbird hawk-moths move their wings so fast, they emit an audible hum. At first, I thought it was one of those giant, fat bumblebees that coast lazily about flowerbeds, seemingly drunk on nectar as they bump and bumble their way through the plants. But then it zipped out from underneath the dusky pink flowers, and I was taken aback by its ginormous size (their wingspan can be over 50mm, which makes it a bit of a beast in moth terms) and its appearance. It was almost cartoonish; a great furry body and thick, fuzzy feelers, with two markings on the head that looked like the wide eyes of a Disney character. And of course, that delightfully ridiculous appendage, the proboscis. Its wings were a blur of orange as it moved about the honeysuckle in rapid, jerky movements, and I could certainly see where the name had come from. Once satisfied, the moth zoomed off to attend to other important business, leaving its buzz to reverberate around the tombstones.

Pick your way through the grassland, and you come to the real wilderness. Directly behind the church, nature has truly taken its course. The trees, as if in payback, have grown wonderfully crooked, their branches hanging low over the path as they reach across to their nearest neighbour. They form a dense canopy that envelops everything in a cloak of muted, emerald light and the heady scent of damp earth, so thick and close it appears to block out any sounds

A red admiral butterfly sunning itself.

Ivy overtakes a tombstone.

of the outside world. Everything is covered in a deep blanket of ivy, the waxy leaves over-running the tombstones and crawling up the tree trunks. Some trees had been completely taken over; thick vines draped over their boughs and dangled over the ground, a slightly demurer version of the gnarled, twisted lianas that hang across the great trees in the deep jungles of the tropics. Enormous bushes of holly join the ivy, so that the whole scene looks like a rather over-enthusiastic Christmas card. I've spent many a festive season here, walking off the calories by taking pictures with numbing fingers. Winter lends an almost magical feeling to it; the ivy frosted and sparkling, the spider webs decorated with glittering baubles of water-droplets. Towards the end of winter, little clusters of snowdrops collect around the base of trees, their ivory buds breaking up the continuous carpet of green. And in spring, daffodils sprout their proud yellow trumpets in defiance, heralding the beginning of a brand-new season.

Around the corner is summer, where those honeysuckle bushes creep over the walls and wild garlic grows in abounds, releasing its cloying scent. In the warmth, this smell seems to get trapped within the thick foliage and even the bees stagger about drunkenly, bumping into branches and monuments with a disgruntled buzz. As for the tombstones themselves, they are barely recognisable. Weather-beaten and almost sanded bare, the crumbling facades are now coloured mustard yellow and dirty white by lichens, and decorated with the skeletons of ivy past.

And with all this plant life, inevitably, come animals. As well as the hawk-moth, I've seen a great variety of insects, from spiders with abdomens the size of my thumb to tiny, scarlet ones little bigger than a pinhead, strung about the rough stone walls like fairy lights. Amongst the grass are ladybirds of every colour – cherry red and shiny, lemon yellow with pale brown spots, great fat tangerine ones with dark splodges. My favourite was a Hallowe'en inspired character, a shiny black button with orange spots making her way up

A thick bush of holly.

Daffodils in the spring.

the side of a particularly decrepit grave stone. Amazingly, there are around 5,000 species of ladybugs across the world, and they are little ecological gems. They naturally control the numbers of agricultural pests, like aphids, so effectively that some gardeners swear by them, even believing them 'lucky'.

And of course, with insects come the birds. Coal tits, plump and characterful in their little miner's caps, squabbled over the spoils of a lone bird feeder hung by the church, the peanuts strewn across the grass. Once I caught a fleeting glimpse of a woodpecker, his speckled plumage just visible as he flitted round the other side of the tree trunk. In spring, the graveyard becomes the perfect contradiction; alive with activity. Lady blackbirds, who confusingly are a dull brown, scrabble noisily in the undergrowth. Robins and wrens perform the dawn chorus, while chiff-chaffs huff tunefully to one another. I once stumbled across a chaffinch, who hastily disappeared into a thicket of trees, looking slightly stressed and ruffled. Emanating from the thicket was the unmistakeable, relentless chirping of young in a nest – and now I understood the distinctive, panicked air only a new father could have. Not wanting to disturb them I didn't venture into the thicket, but it made me smile all the same. That same day I also ran

Ghosts of lichens past.

Ladybird sitting in the grass.

into a stoat, its slender, mahogany body rigid and poised to escape at any given moment. We exchanged fleeting, surprised glances, before it wriggled off into the thick tangle of brambles from which it came.

As the sun sets and twilight sets in, a new set of wildlife comes out to play. Bats make an appearance and one evening I came to find another infamous character: a tawny owl. Earlier that day, a friendly dog-walker alerted me to an individual that had set up camp in an artificial nest box in the bottom right corner of the graveyard. I headed down just as the sun came down, on a hazy summer evening filled with moths and scatty daddy long-legs. I successfully located the nest box; a wee triangular, pine-wood box nailed high up on an oak tree, facing out into the horses' field next door. But no owl! I sat and waited until the sky turned inky black, smattered with stars, but gradually started to feel a little creeped out sitting with my back to a graveyard, and decided to call it. Just as I reached the tiny gap in the hedge where I would normally squeeze through to reach the path, I heard it. A loud, high-pitched woo, echoing through the night and clear as crystal. Two, hiccupping notes, followed by a series of shorter ones in a juddering rhythm. It truly was a ghostly sound, cutting through the muggy air like a knife through butter. The hairs on the back of my neck stood up and tingled. Eventually, the call receded as the tawny vanished on his nightly hunt, and I made my way home guided by the pearly light of the moon.

These type of places – where nature has reclaimed what was previously lost – are often, to me, the most magical. They have a peaceful air. In the graveyard, plant and animal life are quite happy to work with what we gave them, a bit like us restoring an old house back to its former glory; a nice wee reminder that life always comes full circle.

Gardens part 1: feathered lessons

The first bird I ever properly learnt to identify was a goldfinch. I was around the age of five, sitting cross-legged on the rug in our living room. It had been one of those long, boring days trapped inside by an interminable rain, that made time drag itself pathetically from one endless hour to the next. It was the most frustrating type of weather - rain that couldn't even be bothered to do it properly, but instead fell in fine sheets of miserable drizzle. There was nothing I hated more than being confined to the walls of the house and I spent these days drifting between being a nuisance to my family, playing intense games on the carpet or standing in the porch with my nose snubbed up against the glass, staring forlornly at the damp outdoors and wishing for the rain to stop. My parents were firm advocates that a little bit of rain never hurt anybody, but as I was a child who staunchly refused to wear a coat and had the ability of attracting mud, like a magnet, I was my own worst enemy.

I had been playing with my toys – quietly for once – on the carpet, but had drifted off into a daydream, looking out of our front window. There are two trees outside our house; a short, chubby conifer in the shape of an obese triangle, and a skeletal mountain ash. In September, the latter would herald the arrival of autumn with clusters of waxy, crimson berries, which attracted a variety of birds. I was jerked out of my daze by the arrival of the most colourful birds I'd ever seen. They were decked out in circus colours, with shining golden bodies and jet-black wings, decorated with white speckles and banana yellow patches. Their faces were scarlet masks painted onto white heads with a striking black band across the eyes, so that they looked like a cross between circus performers and Spanish bandits. The pair fluttered and twirled about the peeling silvery bark of the tree and I soon became enraptured by these vibrant acrobats, so much so that I failed to realise the sky had brightened considerably. I turned to the oracle on all matters – my dad – and asked him what these things were.

"Goldfinches," He said without pause, peering over the top of a book. "Pretty little things."

From then on, I smugly pointed out any goldfinch I came across, to anyone who would listen, filled with pride at my newly acquired knowledge. A few months later, during a lesson on 'garden wildlife', we had to identify some common birds from some ancient flashcards, yellowed from years of rough handling by sticky fingers. When the teacher held up a familiar golden image, I almost burst with the answer.

"It's a goldfinch!" I cried, jumping out my seat, before adding, "pretty little things."

Our gardens – whatever size, shape or type they may be – are the perfect example of how you don't have to travel far to see and appreciate wildlife. Whether well-manicured or tangled overgrown jungle; gravelled with a few lonely potted plants or stuffed to bursting with flowers and shrubs, you'll be able to find wildlife in some shape or form. Gardens can be a hive of activity, and it was in gardens that my insatiable appetite for learning about animals was spawned.

As a family, we had various gardens that featured heavily in my childhood. Our own garden was small but mighty; my parents were both avid gardeners and this wee space was crammed with a huge variety of plants, from towering roses that drooped over the path to squat little patches of pansies. The tiny paved section was bordered by pots that harboured my mam's herb garden (which she still cultivates to this day) and a broad, wooden shelf filled with my dad's private obsession: bonsais. I was always fascinated by these perfect miniature replicas, an oriental garden transported into our little back yard. However, they are notoriously fickle plants, and the flourishing growth of our collection could only be attributed to my dad's fastidious system of care, carefully crafted over the years. As such I was not allowed to touch them, so instead I studied the insects that crawled over them from a safe distance.

Much of my young life was spent in this garden. My mam is one of those heroic people who devoted her life to nursing, and used to be in bed for most of the day after a long night on the ward. This meant my dad – who retired when I was young – had the equally heroic task of keeping me quiet and entertained. This was quite a feat, given the most commonly used phrase in my school report was 'chatterbox' closely followed by 'can't sit still'. The garden was the perfect solution. He had fingers greener than the plants he tended to, and could happily while away the hours pottering about and nurturing things; whereas I could combine my favourite pastimes of poking about in search of animals and getting as dirty as possible. I'm sure I probably got underfoot most of the time, but my dad never seemed annoyed. In fact, he taught me so much during these times. I would besiege him with an endless stream of questions, which he would answer the best he could – and on the rare occasion he couldn't, we'd consult the extensive catalogue of Reader's Digest volumes stacked on the landing.

It was here I learnt that everything had a place; every living thing had a job and importance in the world, and therefore everything needed to be treated with respect. I was taught to observe, not intrude, how to pick things up gently and replace them back where they came from. How to lift stones to reveal the thronged cities of insect life underneath, how to approach birds without scaring them away and to rub the thick leaves of herbs with my finger and thumb to release their scent. It was also here that I cultivated a tendency to give animals personalities. When I entered the world of serious scientific study, I was told firmly that the personification of wildlife was wrong, but (as you can probably tell from this book) I am still unable to look at an animal without giving it a voice, a personality, and a back story. It may not be strictly scientific, but it makes life more fun...

Perhaps some of the easiest animals to attribute personalities to are garden birds, which we all know and love. Different species of tit, for example, demonstrate different attitudes to life. Blue tits come across as energetic little busybodies, never still for long but instead flitting from branch to branch, or clinging onto a violently swinging bird feeder upside-down. Their distinctive sky-blue plumage from which they get their name seems to get brighter come breeding season, mixed with lemon yellow and pale green – the colours of spring. They are dainty little birds, with miniscule beaks used to peck efficiently at seeds and a skittish way of movement. I once

Blue tit.

Blue tit female emerging from the nest.

A great tit. This picture was taken whilst ringing garden birds for University.

came across a hard-working mother, who had nested in a crack in the trunk of a young oak tree. She would appear at the entrance, head twitching in all directions as she made a rapid assessment of the dangers. Satisfied there were no significant threats, she would burst out of the tree and out into the nearby hedgerow in search of food. For a few minutes, she would be gone and I could sneak a peek inside the little crack – and there, just visible, were two chicks, fuzzy with down. Upon her return, the female would land on a tree some distance away, carefully surveying her environment, before proceeding to dart to the next tree closest, and then the next, always pausing at each stop to check she hadn't been followed. Finally, she would arrive at the nest tree, give a few darting glances about, and vanish back into the crack, her vivid blue colouring disappearing into the gloom. Barely a minute later, she would appear again to repeat the whole process – it was knackering just watching her!

If blue tits are the over-zealous mothers of the family, then great tits are the bullying cousins. As the name suggests they are the largest species of tit, and I have often seen them muscle their way into the crowds at a bird table and chase off the smaller ones. Their colouring is duller by comparison; where the blue-tit has a vivid blue cap on the crown of the head, the great tit has a black one. Their Latin name, Parus major, seems in line with their behaviour – the bossiness at the bird table, the rather determined swagger they adopt when scouring the garden for food or nest material. I even saw one tearing the luminous green fuzz off my dog's tennis ball, at which he was most affronted.

If you're lucky enough to have a garden, or a window that looks out onto one, you can learn a lot by just sitting and watching the coming and goings of bird life. My early life as a Zoologist was spent just watching the drama unfold in our own back garden, or those of my grandparents. My grandma and granddad, who lived just across the road, had an even tinier space than ours, completely concrete. The only plant life came from a few cracked pots with faded purple hydrangeas and a towering hedge that bordered the garden, and prevented the neighbours from getting 'too nosy' (this didn't stop the gossip-loving lady next door, who used to hitch up her skirts and climb onto an upturned pot to peer over the wall). But it made up for its lack of vegetation in the sheer amount of birds. My grandparents were great bird lovers and would feed them fastidiously throughout the year, the walls adorned with tiny bird houses and every available surface scattered with breadcrumbs. My granddad was a keen carpenter, and he erected bird tables taller than me, with little slanted roofs like the chocolate box houses of the Swiss alps. He also had the fantastic hobby of sitting quietly on their stone bench, and ever so slowly coaxing blackbirds to feed out of his hand. I was transfixed by this witchcraft, sitting at his feet with rapt attention. I got a real close-up look at blackbirds; their sleek, black feathers, glossy and dark as ink, their beady eyes ringed with sulphur yellow to match their beak. I loved the careful way they selected the perfect crumb from his outstretched palm, before swooping off to the top of the wall to enjoy it properly. Sometimes they'd even give us a burst of musical song, by way of thanks.

And it wasn't just blackbirds that were regular visitors to my grandparents' tiny concrete paradise. Sparrows amassed in the vast hedge, chattering noisily to one another. Walking past, you were greeted with a wall of sound; chirping, chirruping and eventually a great rustling of wings as they exploded out of the leaves as one body. Another great mass of birds came in the form of starlings, who descended on the bird feeders and tables in great numbers. My grandma despised them, and called them 'great brutes' on account of their boisterous table manners. But I thought they were gorgeous birds; their silky, iridescent black feathers shone emerald-violet in the light, and were covered in a smattering of tiny, white specks. To me, it's almost like seeing a galaxy in bird form – they are the David Bowie to the blackbird's Johnny Cash.

And starlings do something else that is out of this world. They roost in enormous colonies, in places tucked away from predators – this can be woodland, but also industrial structures such as the roof spaces of factory buildings, and underneath bridges. At dusk, as the

Chaffinch high up in a blossom tree.

flock returns from a hard day gathering food, they pause at the skyline above the roost and perform one of nature's most stunning aerial displays. Thousands of individuals, swooping and swirling in unison like a great, seething mass of black in the sky, shifting in shape in an almost hypnotic fashion. This amazing feat is called a murmuration. We used to have a murmuration of starlings in Aberdeen, roosting beneath a bridge right in the middle of the city. I remember leaning on a lamp-post at sunset and watching this incredible eruption of birds move like a swirling, liquid mass.

It's not known exactly why starlings do this. A popular theory is that it confuses predators; the ever-shifting shapes making it hard to pinpoint an individual, confuddling the brains of the likes of peregrine falcons. It's also thought they gather to exchange information and touch base with one another after a long day apart, before tucking themselves in a huddled warmth for the night. But I can tell you on good authority – I've been to many different parts of the world, yet a murmuration of starlings is still high on my list of wildlife spectaculars.

Back in my dad's more exotic, plant-filled garden across the road, a greater variety of birds passed through, probably attracted by the myriad insects that visited his flowers. Finches – small, rotund birds with arched, pointed wings and triangular bills – occupied various niches of the garden. Chaffinches would often choose to avoid the heavy crowds at the bird feeders and instead scrape about under bushes and shrubs, the males conspicuous for their reddish-pink breast and pale grey head. They share the white flashes on the wing and outer tail feathers with the duller coloured female, and sport a broad, sharp beak, the colour of steel. Their call to me is synonymous with summer; a cheerful, rousing song, with varied twittering riffs. Bullfinches are also regulars, and look like a butch version of the chaffinch – their pink breast slightly more pronounced, their cheeks the same, ruddy colour. In contrast to the greyish head of its smaller counterpart, the bullfinch has a rather macho, jet-black head, that gives him the impression of a furrowed brow, and a stubbier, thicker beak. They feed voraciously on the young buds of trees, hopping about the branch determinedly and showing off their white rumps. However, the bullfinches call is a mournful, melancholy sound, that belies their 'hard-man' appearance.

Watching the daily activity in the garden challenged my perceptions of certain species. The robin, for example, was for a long time a Thing That Signalled The Start of Christmas, alongside my mam obsessively feeding the demanding monster that was the Christmas cake in the freezer with rum and the musty, artificial scent of last year's tinsel. A huge revelation in my youth was that these birds were not restricted to the festive season, but in fact were present all year round – it was just that their magnificent cherry red breast did not stand out so much against the greenery of the other seasons. They were often in our garden, hopping about sweetly or giving enigmatic performances as night fell and the street lamps began to glow. But through watching their behaviour intently, I began to realise something else about robins: they aren't all sugar and spice. They are – officially I believe – the nation's favourite garden bird, with their delicate beaks, decidedly cute faces and iconic appearance. However, when

Robin in the garden.

it comes to personal space, they can become extremely territorial and will aggressively drive away any intruder. I once saw a robin see off a cheeky magpie that had landed to take advantage of the titbits we'd scattered, running towards it stiff-legged with wings held aloft, its crimson chest almost glowing in fury. Robins are one of the few bird species who hold territories all year round, and our garden often became an arena for males to compete. They would begin by singing loudly at one another, and attempting to perch higher and higher in an effort to show off more effectively. Although all the disputes I saw were settled by this method, these fights can even escalate to the death – a furious battle for space and, most importantly, the ladies.

Once a couple has been established, they will guard the male's territory together. We once had a pair who staked their claim at the back of our garden which, unfortunately, was directly below the bird feeder we had suspended from the crooked old tree that hunched over the back wall. In some respects, this was clever; an everlasting supply of food, a great stone bench under which to shelter from bad weather. But it also received the highest number of visitors to the garden, and as such the couple were far from marital bliss. Instead, they were permanently fraught with worry and outrage at the various intruders that entered this territory throughout the day. And when we appeared to refill the bird feeder, the male would descend into abject panic, hopping from foot to foot and singing loudly at us. Apparently, our slight height advantage did not deter him.

There is another garden bird that is, perhaps, more numerous in urban spaces than any other. But unlike the robin and the blackbird, this one lacks any iconic features, is never said to be cute or beautiful, and has a fair few annoying habits. I am of course, talking about the pigeon.

These birds became an annual source of annoyance for me, because every single year – usually around exam time – they would begin courtship. My bedroom was an extension of the garage with a flat roof, and it also looked over onto the slanted conservatory roof of the house behind. Both these spaces were the favourite haunts of pigeons, who liked nothing better but to settle comfortably and coo incessantly. If you were sitting at your desk attempting to revise it was akin to Chinese water torture. And then at night, once the bleating call had finally become background noise and was almost lulling you to sleep, the pigeons would decide to have a late-night party and would scrabble about on the roof, their feet scraping unbearably against the tarmac. Admittedly, I was not the best at concentrating, but the antics of amorous pigeons haunted my education from my GCSEs right through to my final uni exam.

There was one particular individual who seemed to return every year. Don't ask how I knew it was her – she just had a unique air about her. She reminded me of a retired opera singer; the type who no longer perform and spend their days reclined on squashy velvet sofas devouring chocolates, but still demonstrate very diva-ish tendencies. She was the fattest pigeon I'd ever seen, and would painstakingly waddle her way about the conservatory roof before settling in the perfect spot. When she squatted down, her body spread across the tiles like melted butter, and great rolls would form around her neck. As if to add to the illusion, she would ruffle out her plumage extravagantly, so that the end result was like a deflated football covered with feathers. In my mad, revision-addled brain, I named her Madame, and she became a huge source of both procrastination and amusement.

Pigeons must like their ladies on the larger side of life, and Madame was never short of gentlemen callers. The males would arrive in droves, pushing and shoving one another, jostling for space on the peak of the roof behind. Madame would appear not to notice this sudden onset of testosterone, instead taking long, deep breaths, visibly expanding with every one. I almost expected her to produce a tiny fan and begin wafting herself with it. Eventually, one male (usually the biggest and most experienced) would work up the courage to swoop down and land on the conservatory roof a few feet away from Madame, where he would attempt to look casual by pacing up and down like an army marshal. Apparently, Madame believed his laid-back persona and looked entirely disinterested. He then began to coo softly, purring low with his neck feathers puffed out like an Elizabethan ruff. The other males were still lined up on the roof behind, and I could practically hear them egging him on. She however, seemed bored by this display, so he upped the ante – thrusting out his chest, his coos became louder and more dramatic. Still, she ignored him. His efforts became more desperate, until eventually he was cooing with such passion that his eyes were popping. His stride developed into some sort of erratic march, and the 'lads' up on the roof were practically bobbing with excitement. The object of his affections, however, closed her eyes and settled in for a little nap.

I felt a bit sorry for these males. They tried so hard, often to no avail. Madame was clearly a hard lady to please, fussy about her men and as such, scathingly indifferent toward those who did not fit the bill. Sometimes, the pigeons would just give up and fly away disheartened. The unwise (or disillusioned, perhaps) would carry on approaching Madame and try it on with her, to which she would

Wren.

become quite annoyed and launch a furious attack, almost pecking their eyes out. When the right suitor did arrive, however, she would become different, leaping (slowly) to her feet and returning their enamoured coos with great purring ones. I could practically see her batting her eyelashes (if she had any, that is ... birds don't have eyelashes per se). I became so familiar with Madame that if any of these courtship rituals ended happily, I would close my curtains out of respect. Pigeons deserved privacy, even if they did insist on doing it on a roof.

Another familiar species is the wren. Wrens are minute, dumpy birds, who usually hold their short tails cocked vertically as they hop endearingly about the ground in search of their favourite spiders and insects. For this purpose, their beak is narrower than most finches, and they lack the colourful plumage of the chaffinch or bullfinch instead decorated in cappuccino colours of brown and cream. But they are the Ariana Grandes of the bird world; tiny, but with enormous voices. Their lyrical song penetrates through windows, and can be heard loud and clear first thing on a summer's morning. Speaking of song ... early one autumn we were frequented by another musician; a song thrush. In the early morning, when the dew was still sparkling amongst the blades of grass, it would sing its heart out from atop the wall at the back of our garden. Looking out through the curtains, I would watch it standing proud and straight on its gangly pink legs, its pale chest puffed out to show the delicate spotting. Its musical song it similar to that of blackbirds, but can be distinguished by the fact that the thrush repeats the same short phrases, over and over again, like a broken record. I would often see it again later in the morning, engaged in the slightly more brutal act of smashing snails against rocks by jerking its head, breaking into their shells to release the tender meat inside. Sadly, the song thrush is declining rapidly, affected by changes to agricultural practices.

And it's not just the song thrush. Severe decline is a trend we're seeing across many of our common garden species. Great murmurations of starlings are becoming a rarer sight; their population crashing due to a loss of permanent pasture – their preferred habitat – and the general intensification of livestock rearing. House sparrows have shown one of the greatest declines of all our garden birds over the last twenty years, with London alone demonstrating a 60 per cent decline in numbers. It is thought this is due to a lack of invertebrate prey for youngsters, coupled with a loss of available nesting sites in towns and cities. Both these species are now red-listed. Many garden birds are susceptible to particularly cold, harsh winters, and may suffer brief fluctuations in population size as a result. But, remembering that they face other threats – thanks to changes in agriculture, and the way we build and expand our houses – we need to make an extra effort to help them out, and encourage these birds to our gardens to nest and fatten up during the colder months.

Our garden birds can be wonderful to observe and enjoy. You will see feeding frenzies and arguments over titbits found on bird tables, territorial stand-offs and brawls over potential partners. The more tender moments include the interactions between busy parents as they hastily gather nest material, or as they flit backwards and forwards between the nest to feed their ever-hungry offspring. Or there is the sweet harmony of many different species enjoying a bird bath, splashing and fluffing out their feathers. You can also earmark the seasons by watching the birds. Coy couples flirt during spring, followed by frantic parenting; tentative fledglings stumble about in summer and a chorus of song floats from the hedgerow. And as the bounty of summer gives way to the famine of autumn and winter, feeding stations become filled with birds of all shapes and sizes. And the best thing? Even if the rain keeps you trapped indoors, you can still enjoy all of this – you don't even have to move from your sofa.

Gardens part 2: Marvellous minibeasts

Gardens have so much wildlife in them I had to split this chapter into two, and I couldn't not include a piece about insect life. The fact is, most of the wildlife in our gardens – and of the whole world, actually – is made up of invertebrates. For example, insects outnumber humans by 250, 000 to 1, and there are over 21,000 types in the UK alone. But despite completely overtaking us in numbers, these creatures often go unnoticed and are vastly under-appreciated, labelled as 'creepy-crawlies' and either seen as something disgusting, horrifying or just downright annoying. Flicking ants off our picnic table, swatting at flies or swiping at wasps, we rarely take the chance to stop and reflect on how important these tiny beings are. But gardens are filled with all manner of miniscule super-heroes, essential not just for the health of your small patch of earth, but of the whole planet. So here it is, an ode to the marvellous minibeast.

I don't know at what point in life insects become unfavourable. The point where childish curiosity gives way to the squirming, squeamish adulthood; where we stop collecting things in jars and scooping critters up to crawl across the palm of our hand, often accompanied by a handful of soil to be smeared on your clothes later. Some insects – for reasons only known to us – are more acceptable than others. The butterfly, for instance, is always seen as something pretty and harmless, whereas its equally fluttery cousin the moth is viewed by some with irritation as they bang relentlessly into a lamp. Bees are fuzzy and friendly, yet wasps are mean-spirited, evil beasts, hell bent on stinging everything in sight. Earthworms and slugs are described as slimy and squirming, but put a shell on the latter and it's just a friendly old snail. But, as I explained earlier, the gardens of my childhood taught me that everything had an important place in the world, a vital function that kept the environmental cogs turning – no matter how small, or mean, or ugly. I developed a profound respect for everything – even the things that made me shudder a little inside.

One animal that always gives me nightmares is the spider. It would be wrong of me to deny this fact, especially as my family would be the first to call me out on it. I've worked with animals far bigger, far scarier, and way more venomous, but the completely harmless spiders of our home country? They put the fear of God into me. My family take great joy in telling anyone who will listen that right up until my teens, if one so much as put a leg inside my bedroom, I would stand at the top of the stairs, shaking all over and screaming for someone to come and rescue me from this formidable beast. As I got older, this progressed to putting a glass over them, then pacing the room until I plucked up the courage to slide some card underneath and put it outside (or until a braver soul came along and did it for me). Even now, I can't so much as look at a picture of one without feeling itchy all over. Luckily, my Dad also drilled into me the importance and brilliance of spiders, so I can still admire them … albeit from a safe distance. Even if it does mean I'm left in a conundrum every time I see one, torn between wanting it gone and concern for its well-being (I'm emotionally drained by the time it's disappeared).

Despite finding the actual spider visually unappealing, I never tire of their webs. They are beautiful, intricate feats of natural architecture, and spiders are masters of their craft. I used to love watching them weave their web, their multiple legs working in double time as they went about their fiddly task, like the needles of an industrial sewing machine. The way they do it is amazing. The spider will begin by casting out a shimmering line of silk into the air so that it catches the wind, carrying it across to the nearest tree or branch; once secured, it will then make a bridge between this and the beginning point, creating a 'v' shape. It will then make another

bridge, and another, building out slowly from the core and attaching more and more threads to the anchor points. They seem to do this so rapidly, yet so faultlessly – each thread perfectly placed, the pattern so geometrically satisfying. And each species has its own signature style. Orb webs are the classic, circular 'wheel-with-spokes' that we are so familiar with, and can be enormous in size. The biggest I've ever seen belonged to a surprisingly small spider that lived between the gooseberry bushes in my nan's back garden and was bigger than me, aged eight, with my arms outstretched. He (or, more likely, she) would sit so proudly in the middle, the arachnid equivalent of an architect of skyscrapers, and wait patiently for the vibrations that would travel across the carefully placed lines to signify the arrival of dinner. I was sure she must catch more flies than any other spider, although it would be a mammoth undertaking just to travel over to retrieve those that had become trapped around its boundary.

Another kind are 'cobwebs', which contrary to popular belief are not blown easily away by the wind. They refer to the masses of sticky, candyfloss tangles that collect in attic corners, or the windows of neglected sheds, often concealing a bunch of eggs. 'Funnel' webs appear to have required more planning, and consist of a carefully constructed tunnel with a hole running through the middle inside which a sly spider lies in wait. And sheet webs are, as the name suggests, a wide, flat sheet of silk, with its owner residing patiently underneath. I always feel the utmost admiration for the creatures that create these, and the amount of time and effort that go into the craft. My favourite time of year is when the cooler weather sets in, and the silk becomes barbed with droplets of dew so that they sparkle about the garden, like strings of fairy lights hung across the bushes. In the still quiet of dawn, they lend a magical quality, the silvery threads glittering in the pale pink light of early morning.

They may seem fragile, but spider silk is stronger than steel. Its elastic qualities make it incredibly durable – have you ever noticed, if you walk through one accidentally, that it doesn't break apart, but clings to your clothes and skin? And spider silk isn't just used for indestructible shelters and booby traps. Spiders are the only animal that produce different silks for different purposes; it is a multi-functional tool. The bolas spider attaches a sticky blob onto the end of a line of silk, and casts it out into the air to catch any unsuspecting flies, like a fisherman. Jumping spiders parasail using their silk, leaping up into the air then holding up a sort of parachute to prolong their flight. Fellow arachnophobes; although jumping spiders sound terrifying, in the UK they are only teeny tiny (growing up to around 8mm) and are, I must admit, kind of cute. The zebra jumping spider is one of our species, given its name due to its black and white striped body, and happens to be little and fuzzy.

Another silk function includes communication. Spider conversation consists of a series of silk 'trails' left behind them on their travels, and sex is usually the language spoken (sex is the main talking point of the animal kingdom in general). The females lace their threads with pheromones to entice potential mates, and these chemical signals can be so detailed that a possible conquest can decipher her relationship history, including how many exes she has. I suppose with spiders, honesty is the best policy – best to lay it all out on the table so there are no surprises later – unless you are a species like the black widow or raft spider, in which case you're likely to be eaten shortly afterward. As well as being the femme fatales of the minibeast world, spiders are also forward thinking in another respect: recycling. They'll often consume a web at the end of the day to conserve silk, recycling it the next morning when they build a fresh new one.

It only stands to reason that if there are many different types of web and many different purposes for them, then there are countless species of spider. There are enormous predators that stalk in the drains, thick of body and thick of leg (my least favourite), miniscule ones so thin they are almost transparent (my favourite) and all manner of shapes and sizes in between. There are two kinds of spider I can get along with; garden and money spiders. I became almost pally with garden spiders as I 'helped' my dad (if 'helped' means get underfoot and pull bits off things), mostly because they kept themselves to themselves, suspended in the bullseye of their orb web. They usually hung upside down so that their fat, almond-shaped abdomen pointed skywards and their long legs curved around their bodies. I also liked their interesting markings; easily identifiable due to the white cross located on the back. They come in a whole range of colours, from rich, chocolate brown to bonfire orange, and one autumn both my dad and I were surprised by an explosion of miniature yellow spiders, that seemed to spill out from the branches of our tree. We later discovered that these were the spiderlings of my favourite species, which I'd taken to calling 'hot-cross bun spiders'.

The second kind I could cope with was the money spider, those tiny, black souls that normally descend in front of your eyes from the ceiling, like burglars performing an intricate heist. Perhaps it's their minute size, or the superstition that they will bring you good fortune, but I've always found these spiders to be distinctly friendly. And at just over 250 species, they make up a third of all spiders in the UK, which should be reassuring for arachnophobes – that's a lot of good fortune!

In our house, the autumn months were benchmarked by one critter in particular. As soon as the leaves began to fall and the air turned cooler, we would be plagued by a persistent, mechanical chirp that emanated from our airing cupboard. It was too loud to be ignored, and so repetitive it drove you to near madness – much like the incessant cooing our pigeon colony had caused us to endure all summer. But it was no bird that made this noise. For if you opened the door and peered inside, there, perched atop a mountain of fluffy towels, would be a grasshopper. Realising he'd been discovered, the culprit would cease making noise and freeze, fixing you with a stare of horror. Grasshoppers have a brilliantly comical face, long and flat with two large, cartoonish eyes – although of course, these eyes aren't as they appear. All insects have 'compound' eyes, which consist of numerous tiny lenses all clubbed together instead of just one. It just so happens that the round, bulbous eyes of the grasshopper are often pale in colour, with a darker spot towards the middle just like a pupil, the result being that the insect always looks permanently over-excited or terrified (depending on how you look at it). This comical look isn't helped by the fact that the mouthparts overlap in such a way that they give the impression of a crazed grin. I would always open the door to a slightly maniacal-looking individual, its antennae twitching imperceptibly and eyes wide in shock.

Up close and personal, we'd get a good look at the offending instrument: their two back legs, folded in a high arch behind them, sinewy and elongated. Closer inspection revealed many rows of stubby hair-like structures. That pulsing chirp is created by the grasshopper rubbing these 'pegs' together – a 'stridulation', to give

the fancy technical term. Loud choruses of grasshoppers can be heard emulating from thick patches of grass and shrubs throughout the mating season in August and September, as the male plays enthusiastically to attract a female. I don't exactly know why our airing cupboard was such an attractive arena for these enigmatic performers – perhaps the warmth and comfort was an attractive prospect as opposed to busking in the crisp air outside. But our visitors never seemed to have any luck. They were always lone singletons, driving us insane with their hopeful song, and for about a week there would be an endless stream of them. No sooner had we removed one and breathed a collective sigh of relief, there would be another in its place; a rapid succession of main acts and understudies.

If you want to really appreciate the importance of minibeasts, look no further than the darkest, dampest corners of your garden. I'm talking that pile of rotting leaves, the dark crevice between the plant pots where no-one goes, the compost heap with its musty, tangy scent of earth and fermented foliage. For deep below the ground reside some of our most vital ecosystem cogs, squirming, wriggling and crawling to their hearts content.

Nan and Poppa had a brilliant garden. It was an exceptionally long, rectangular space that backed onto the local Metro line; here, the passage of time was signalled by the rumble and rattle of the trains as they passed every twenty minutes. It was vastly different to Dad's carefully tended garden because it had the benefit of space; to avoid clutter, everything in our garden had its place, but this one was a great mismatch of habitats. And where Dad nurtured bonsais, Poppa cultivated food – little clumps of strawberry plants, decorated with their protective cloches of mesh and plastic; a dense collection of gooseberry bushes that stood in rows, like a miniature vineyard. The spiky shards of onions would sprout from the ground, the bulbs just peeking out from their bed of soil alongside the limp, veiny leaves of brassicas. And rhubarb – some of the biggest specimens I've ever seen – their flat, paddle-like leaves drooping over the lawn.

My weekends were mostly spent on my hands and knees, uprooting potatoes dusted with earth or collecting the marbled green gooseberries for endless crumbles and jams. Working in such close proximity to the soil meant I had able opportunity to observe some of the beasties that lived in it, and I would constantly forget my tasks in favour of lying on my stomach in the dirt and watching. It was here, for example, I discovered earth worms – an inevitable point in childhood. Digging a little over-enthusiastically with my plastic trowel I would usually unearth some poor individual, which I would pick up with exaggerated gentility and place in the palm of my hand.

The worm would writhe about in outrage (or panic, it's very hard to gauge the emotions of worms), twisting and turning its salmon coloured body. I was fascinated by them. The skin was so paper-thin it was almost transparent, and I could see the digestive tract digesting the soil it had been munching on before it was so rudely interrupted. Sometimes, the worm would have a fat saddle around its middle, paler than the rest of its body. I later learnt that this was known as a 'clitellum', a multi-functional organ that served as a reproductive organ and, later, an egg cocoon, from which the tiny eggs would spill when the time was right. Saddled or no, I would always replace the worm to exactly where I found it, and then watch as it returned to its daily business. I loved the way they moved; it was almost like a ripple travelled up and down the worm, its body pulsing as it dug back down into the depths of the earth. I deduced that the pointier end must be the head, as it was always this end that disappeared first.

Earthworms may be completely blind and admittedly, a little ugly, but they are one of the most important beasties out there. As they munch their way through the soil (an unusual diet, I'll admit), they create tunnels through it, which aerates the soil and helps to enrich the earth. They're almost like the bin-men of our planet – helping dead plant material to decompose, keeping the soil clean (well, as clean as soil can be) and healthy. Sometimes, having found a particularly large worm, I would take a dead leaf and leave it enticingly in front of it. Sure enough, the worm would eventually drag the leaf down into the darkness of its tunnel ... it's the only time they could ever look remotely threatening.

Occasionally, I'd strike lucky and it wouldn't be an earthworm in my trowel, but a millipede. These define the term 'creepy crawly' – its very name is derived from the Latin 'mille ped', meaning 'thousand foot'. The millipede's body is made up of countless little segments, each with two jointed legs attached. The end result is a fringing of legs that almost seem to ripple as the creature moves; a motion that always seemed to induce shivers and give me goose bumps. A common species to the UK has the very cool title of the 'black snake', and sports a slim, shiny black to chocolate brown body with a contrasting fringe of white legs (which lend it its other name, the white-legged millipede). Whilst some millipedes can be ferocious predators steaming through the undergrowth like hungry trains, these serve the same purpose as the earthworm, and are quite content nibbling on decaying plant matter. Whenever I'd come across one, it would coil up like a spring almost instantly, in a defensive pose, tucking all those legs in close to its body. I learnt quickly not to pick these up; they don't bite, but release fluid from their sides that carry quite a pungent odour, presumably to deter any birds in search of a tasty snack. The smell remained on my hands for days, much to the disgust of my family.

Of course, there can't be a chapter about garden wildlife without touching on one of my favourite creatures of all time; the bee. Bees have had a great wealth of attention on them in the last decade, mostly because people are waking up to the fact that these wee fuzzy bombardiers are fast disappearing, and that without them we're a little screwed. I am proud to say that my parents' garden was – and still is – a haven for bees. We've always planted 'bee-friendly' herbs and wildflowers. At least four different types of lavender; hollyhocks, foxgloves, poppies, sweet peas and zinnias ensured our garden was filled with a friendly hum throughout spring and summer. And, of course, Mam's fragrant herb garden, with its clusters of sage, thyme and mint.

All kinds of bees frequented our little patch of earth. Some bearing the classic striped pattern we have come to associate with them, some not; some fat and round, some dainty and slender, the gloriously fuzzy to the closely shaven. They came in a range of colours, from black and caramel brown to cinnamon-ginger and golden yellow. I spent many a happy afternoon sitting on the back step, with our reader's digest book open on the 'bee' section and marvelling at the sheer amount of species floating around. I learnt that honeybees are, as the name might suggest, the only type that produce honey as they build their hives. They are not fluffy, but have a shiny, hairless abdomen, striped in bands of dark gold and brown-black. They have sweet, cartoonish eyes and the look of one who is rushed off their feet all day, gathering nectar for a demanding Queen. We also had many different species of bumble-bee; named so for the deep, rumbling buzz they make in flight. We had great, squat ones, coloured a deep chocolate brown and so laden with pollen they'd sway drunkenly from flower to flower. Red-tailed bumblebees sported a bright amber abdomen, like a little beacon, and a fuzzy yellow shrug about the shoulders (I'm not sure if bees have shoulders per se, but bear with the reference). Buff-tailed bumblebees had the more 'classic' bee appearance, with their furry yellow and black stripes, but also large, white fuzzy bottom, like a rabbit's tail. It amused me greatly to find out that the Queen had the largest rump of all – clearly big bottoms are 'in' when it comes to bumblebees.

Solitary bees – the lone wolves of the bee world – tend to look more unusual. Unlike their bumbling and honey-producing cousins, they are not social and live in small burrows underground. They are truly independent women, providing food for their young without the

Bumble bee.

help of worker bees, putting the Queens of hives with their armies of loyal subjects to shame. One species used to greatly annoy my dad by making little semi-circular holes in the leaves of his favourite plants, where they'd taken parts of it back to the nest – the aptly named 'leaf-cutter' bee. These looked suspiciously like honey-bees, except for their vibrant orange underside. They were particularly fond of his prized roses, which on close inspection would be littered with minute discs, as though they'd been attacked by a million miniscule cookie cutters.

As I sat in the sun watching the busy comings and goings of bee-life, I was often visited by hoverflies. These are the friendliest and least

Hoverfly.

disconcerting of flies, hanging effortlessly in the sky and pausing right in front of your face as if to say hello, the lightning-fast speed of their wings giving off a kindly hum. They are the perfect example of something called 'Batesian Mimicry', where a completely harmless animal mimics something more dangerous. Clearly, they are doing a sterling job, as I've seen many a person mistake them for a wasp and quickly vacate the area. They may be striped yellow and black, but they have a flatter, more slender body, and flit between darting and hovering in flight as opposed to the aggressive zig-zag of its stinging doppelganger. Dad taught me a love of hoverflies; as well as bees, they are exceptional pollinators, but also provide natural pest control. For example, the larvae of the cheerfully named 'marmalade' variety will devour damaging aphids, protecting flowers without the need for artificial pesticides.

Bees, hoverflies, moths and butterflies alike all flocked to our enormous buddleia, which towered over the garden like a shaggy umbrella. It's long since been cut down, but in its prime there used to be an insect on every little purple cluster of flowers, and a great deal more hovering around it awaiting their turn. Cabbage white butterflies, with their delicate cream wings and brush-stroke spots fluttered nervously in the queue; red admirals would casually sun themselves, wings folding and unfolding, showing off their striking blue eye spots and black tiger stripes at the wing edge. Tortoiseshell butterflies became almost used to my presence, mistaking my knee for a rock or flower. If I stayed rigidly still, they would land for quite some time, opening their wings to display the orange, black and white colouration from which they get their name, ridged with tiny, sky blue dots.

It goes without saying that most of our garden species are under threat. Bees are declining at an alarming rate, butterflies are becoming a rarer sight – species like the tortoiseshell are being dramatically affected by an increase in parasitic flies like Sturmia bella – and thousands of other species are feeling the pressures of climate change, pesticides, and habitat loss. Even as I return to our little suburban oasis, I can see a change; one or two cabbage whites where there were once twenty, no more grasshoppers using our airing cupboard as a theatre. Make the most of your garden, that little patch you call your own, no matter its size or variety – even a few carefully chosen potted plants on the balcony can make a difference. Look after it and appreciate its residents, for it contains creatures that may just save the planet one day. Not to mention, these creatures can keep eager little minds entertained for hours – so it'll save your sanity as a parent, too.

BIRDS

Food: Garden birds need extra sustenance to see them through the winter months. They like pretty much anything: seeds, nuts, stale breadcrumbs, mealworms, cooked rice...even leftover Christmas pud will do. The only big no-nos are solidified cooking fat, margarine and vegetable oils, desiccated coconut (it may expand inside them) and milk. You can buy good packs of bird seed from your local garden centre, or make your own at home:

An easy recipe for 'fat cakes'

Hanging bird 'cake'.

◆ First up you need a plastic pot – I used an empty humus container, but small yogurt pots work just as well. Make sure it is washed out thoroughly and dry. Then add in a good few dollops (technical terms here…) of nut butter – I used a combination of peanut and almond butter, as I find the consistency of almond butter much better to work with. Then, add in whatever seeds you like; I used sunflower and pumpkin seeds, but any good bird seed will also do. Then a little scattering of dried fruit and give it a good mix around. Some folks also use mealworms at this point too which is a great idea, but if you're a little squeamish they're not a necessity.

◆ Fold a loop of string as a handle and push it deep down into your mixture for a handle. Then pop it in the freezer overnight to harden. In the morning, snip off the plastic covering and you should have a hanging cake!

◆ Whatever you do, make sure the food is on an elevated surface, to keep the birds safe from the local moggies…

Habitat: There are loads of things you can do! Hang bird feeders, erect bird tables and bird baths. Plant native hedgerows, which will provide berries for food and potential nesting habitat. A variety of plants is generally good, from trees to shrubs and climbers such as honeysuckle.

INSECTS

◆ Grow 'bee-friendly' plants, such as lavender, herbs, rudbeckia or salvia ... anything that is pollen-rich

◆ Make a compost heap or leaf pile and cut back on digging to encourage beetles, woodlice and worms. This will also have the added benefit of encouraging amphibians, like toads and newts.

◆ Tie together a bundle of bamboo or thick-stemmed plants, and place in the crack of a wall or tree, to provide nesting habitat for flying insects.

◆ Use as little chemicals as possible – there are natural remedies for pests

◆ Leave at least one area to go completely wild; wildlife loves the messy and unkempt

MAMMALS AND AMPHIBIANS

◆ Make a log pile! Placed in a quiet, damp spot of the garden, you can provide habitat for insects (including bees), frogs, newts and small mammals.

◆ If you want to encourage hedgehogs, form a little tee-pee out of your logs to provide a hedgehog shelter, and place out dishes of water and dog or cat food (never milk or bread, as this can make them ill).

◆ If you have a fence, cut a CD-sized hole out of the bottom of it or dig a tunnel, to allow hedgehogs safe passage.

◆ Create a pond to encourage amphibians. Ponds are just great for wildlife in general – they encourage insects, which provides food for bats and birds, as well as a vital water source.

A final word

There is a common theme throughout this book. The natural world is something to be celebrated; beautiful, interesting, unpredictable, characterful, weird and wonderful. But it is in trouble. Our native species – along with wildlife across the globe – are threatened. Climate change, deforestation, habitat loss, intensive agriculture, pollution, the illegal wildlife trade ... the list of threats is endless. And we're seeing the impacts now – it's not a problem for twenty years' time, or fifty. We're seeing the consequences of these actions today. The facts and figures vary widely, but it's impossible to deny that we are losing species at a higher rate than ever before. The alarming thing is that our planet contains such a rich diversity of species, some we don't even know about yet – species are going extinct without us even knowing about it.

And there is little doubt that we, the human race, are responsible for this rapid increase in extinction rates. Therefore, we have a responsibility to protect what we have left. Wildlife cannot speak for itself – a bee isn't going to fly up to the houses of parliament and say, 'What you're doing is harming us, please stop!' Fish aren't going to begin a clean-up operation of the seas. It's up to us. It can seem like a daunting task, a never-ending news reel of catastrophes and unsolvable issues. But there are many things we can do, from the small every day, to bigger actions. I believe it all begins with a love of nature; finding a joy, passion and care for it. To see it not as a resource, or something that owes us something, but as living beings we share the planet with. There are people that are doing amazing things for the natural world – scientists, broadcasters, campaigners, organisations. And the attitude towards the natural world is changing; more people are re-connecting with nature, and recognising we need to do something now. The green movement is very real. But for most of us, time is an issue. We all have jobs, families, commitments. So how can we help, in our everyday lives, with all the business and worries that go along with having a nine to five? Well, there are many small steps:

1. **Get out an experience nature**. Whether it be in your back garden, or weekend adventures out into the wilds. Appreciate what we have, and the amazing intricacies of our ecosystems. That was the purpose of this book, after all!

2. **Restore and help where you can**. I've added wee bits of advice here and there as to how you can help our hidden wildlife, for example,

These are just a few things that we can do. They aren't herculean tasks, but very important ones. There is a lot of doom and gloom at the moment, but there is also a lot of hope – that together, with the right ingredients, we can save our hidden wildlife.

making your garden wildlife friendly. There are also tonnes of local groups working to improve green spaces and reduce pollution.

3. **Make small changes to reduce waste**. Plastics are one of the biggest issues facing our oceans. **Recycle** responsibly, and limit your use of single-use plastics – **re-use** bags for life, buy unpackaged veg where you can, take your own cutlery (Amazon has some great bamboo cutlery you can use on the go) and use a flask instead of a disposable coffee cup.

4. **Eat less meat**. Simple, but effective. Intensive agriculture – in particular for beef – is environmentally damaging.

5. **Get involved with science:** This could be anything from **volunteering** to **contributing** to initiatives that get you to record what you've seen – all this data goes towards scientific studies. For example, the RSPB's Big Garden Birdwatch, or the University Mammal Challenge.

6. **Write to your local MP** asking what their policies are for nature and the environment, and that they do more to protect it. If enough of us do this, we can have influence. Politicians need votes; if enough of us want something, they need to get it done to survive in politics.

7. **Communicate!** Social media can be a brilliant tool. Connect with others, and communicate the joy of the natural world.

Thank you...

...TO EVERYONE WHO made this book possible. Firstly, to my family and friends – thank you for being so supportive, for the endless cups of tea and words of reassurance, and in some cases for being characters. Thank you to my parents for not just putting up with me, but actively encouraging my crazy endeavours. Thank you to the best adventure buddies anyone could ask for, and special mention to those who delivered their wisdom and took me out on adventures to find the things that fill the pages of this book.

A big thank you to the wonderful team at Pen & Sword, for turning a little blog about wildlife into actual real-life pages. And to my supervisors, for not freaking out when I told you I was going to write a book in the last year of my PhD.

And lastly, thank you to all the wildlife who starred in this book, for giving me such easy material to write about.